About the author

Winnie Salamon began her writing career as a journalist, writing everything from opinion pieces to celebrity gossip for magazines and newspapers including *Marie Claire*, *The SMH*, *The Age* and *NW* where she was once berated by a famous person for asking a shall-not-be named US singer about her celebrity cat-fight. She is the author of *Facetime*, a cult novel that explored geek culture and Internet dating. These days she writes, sews and teaches university students about writing and media. She lives in Melbourne with her husband, two kids, a greyhound, a duck and a couple of geriatric chickens.

Also by Winnie Salamon

Facetime

PRETTY GIRLS DON'T EAT

Winnie Salamon

FORD ST

For Ivy, Fox and Paul. My favourite people.

'Pretty Hurts' – Beyonce

First published by Ford Street Publishing, an imprint of Hybrid Publishers, PO Box 52, Ormond VIC 3204 Australia

www.hybridpublishers.com.au

2 4 6 8 10 9 7 5 3 1

National Library of Australia Cataloguing-in-Publication entry

Creator: Salamon, Winnie, 1976– author.

Title: Pretty girls don't eat / Winnie Salamon.

ISBN: 9781925272772 (paperback)

Subjects: Weight loss – Fiction.

Body image in girls – Fiction.

Career development – Fiction.

Cover design: Cathy Larsen ©

Editor: Robyn Donoghue

Printed in Australia by McPherson's Printing Group

Contents

1: Sometimes Customer Service Is the Last Thing You Want 1
2: Inspired by the Congo 8
3: When Kids Say Your Mum Is a MILF 13
4: Smash Face Sienna 21
5: Never Been Kissed 31
6: Curves: The New Skin and Bone 40
7: Wake Up 49
8: Does the Dog Park Even Count as a Date? 58
9: Pretty Girls Don't Eat 63
10: There's Nothing Like a Good Style Icon to Cheer Up a Girl 67
11: Let's Act Like Nothing Ever Happened 71
12: George Really *Is* Gay 77
13: The Phone Call 80
14: A Normal Loving Family 83
15: Who Needs Chocolate When You Have Praise and Constant External Validation? 88
16: Churn and Burn 92
17: More Than Just Friend Material 95

18: No Cake, Thanks. I'm on a Diet 99
19: Beauty Fades. Dumb Is Forever 105
20: Melody Deserves a Break 109
21: Ramping it Up 113
22: Who Knew Diarrhoea Could Feel So Empowering? 116
23: Fat Is Not a Dirty Word 118
24: My First Client 121
25: Oliver's House 127
26: Best Night of my Life: The Aftermath 131
27: Mix Tape 139
28: Tell it Like it Is 143
29: A Keeper 147
30: You Might Be Dog Ugly, but at Least You're Not Bitter and Twisted 149
31: My Friends Suck 153
32: Don't Try This at Home 160
33: Not Pretty Enough 166
34: Guess What? My Kid's in Hospital 'cos of a Bout of Laxative Abuse 169
35: I Didn't Even Use a Spoon 173
36: How to Achieve a Better Body Image 101 180
37: The Gym 183
38: Out There 191
39: It's Been a Whole Month Since My Last Binge . . . 195
40: Perfect Is Boring 200

Chapter 1: Sometimes Customer Service Is the Last Thing You Want

Call me old-fashioned, but there's nothing quite like a department store in the middle of the week. Quiet, shiny, anonymous. You could spend an entire day in the lingerie section, surrounded by lace, elastic and padded inserts and nobody would consider you a pervert because they wouldn't even notice. Watching the flat screens in electricals, trying out mattresses in bedding, browsing through racks of dresses that cost $2000 each. Applying hand cream, perfume, lipstick. All without a single, 'Can I help you?'

'What do you think?' Melody held up a pair of black pleather leggings. 'Too much?'

'Hmmm . . .' I created a mental picture of Melody, all long shiny black hair, slender limbs, the queen of neutrals, rocking leather. 'Different for you, but I think they could work. Try them on.'

Melody scrunched up her face. 'Oh, okay. We've got time, right?'

'Yes, don't worry. We're not meeting George for another hour.'

While Melody tried on the leggings, I browsed through the new season autumn designer collections. Melody and I never bothered with the basement, where all the markdowns hung messily on over-stuffed racks, sad and dejected as a batch of unwanted kittens. If there's one thing that makes me depressed, it's ill-fitting, poorly constructed, sweatshop produced fashion that nobody wants even when it's half-price. I pulled out my phone and took a picture of a Wedgewood blue lace shift. Looking around to make sure no one was watching, I pulled it off the rack, turned it inside out and photographed the insides. Lazy overlocked seams, and it was $600! Criminal.

'Honest opinion.' Melody came out of the fitting room, barefoot in her leather leggings and oversized white button-up. She looked like an off-duty Hollywood star. Effortless.

'Wow,' I said. 'You look amazing.'

'They're pretty cool. If I was rich I might even buy them.'

'Ha,' I scoffed. 'You don't need to. You've got me.'

'Really? Thanks, Winter, you're the best. I'll totally help you get an A in history.'

Poor Melody. It was the first curriculum day of the year and I knew she felt like she should be in the library studying, but George and I convinced her to spend the day with us. We were only two months into

Year 11 and when school gives you a day off in the middle of the week, it should be embraced.

'Of course you will.' I smiled. 'But you are not allowed to feel guilty for not doing schoolwork today!'

'I know, I know,' Melody said. 'Why did I agree to do final year maths?'

'Because you're brilliant and everyone knows it,' I said. 'Now stand still for a second.'

I took a quick photo, but I didn't really need to. They were just leggings. All I needed to do was find the right fabric and I'd whip up a pair in less than an hour. Melody liked simple silhouettes; I'd sewn half her wardrobe with barely any effort. She always says that one day, when she has money, she'll pay me. But there's no way. Even when we finish high school and university and Melody ends up becoming a successful paediatrician, I'll never accept payment from her.

'See anything good?' she asked.

'I'm kind of into this lace frock. It's cute, don't you think?'

'Gorgeous,' Melody said. 'Very you.'

Unlike Melody, I never try anything on. There's no point. Not many labels go up to my size and even when they do, the fit is usually off. The truth is, I haven't seen the inside of a fitting room for years, not since I was eleven and Mum took me bra shopping.

Talk about being scarred for life.

Mum had made a really big deal out of me

getting my first bra. She had said it was a special occasion so we caught the tram into the city and had lunch at a really fancy place that Mum said served lots of delicious healthy options. We ate tuna niçoise and Mum talked about the time she went into town with Grandma to get her first bra.

'Gosh, I was a 10A. I hardly needed one. Not like now!' She laughed.

The whole thing was pretty embarrassing. But I could tell Mum was trying really hard and that made me feel a bit sorry for her. There I was, getting fatter by the second, and there she was, all glamorous and excited about me getting boobs.

'I think you'll be a 14 something. But we'll get you professionally measured, just to make sure you get enough support for the girls.'

Please, ground, I thought. *Swallow me up*.

Off we went down Bourke Street and into Myer. Mum said hardly anyone shopped here in person anymore, but that it was a really good place to have underwear fitted.

'She's well-developed, isn't she?' remarked the bra lady as she measured my chest.

Thank God I was wearing a singlet.

'It's a beautiful age, when they still have their puppy fat, but they're growing up.'

'Isn't it?' Mum sighed.

My body felt like a piece of meat being inspected to determine whether or not it would be fit for human consumption. I didn't know what to do, so I just stood there in my singlet as the bra lady found me some bras to try on. I thought about all the puppy fat she said I had and how I might be able to get rid of it. I knew, even then, that it wasn't going to disappear all by itself. I'd been scoffing down a lot of chocolate at the time. Puppy fat. *If only*.

While the bra lady searched for bras, Mum chattered away.

'That's the advantage of being a bigger girl,' Mum said. 'The boobs. Not many skinny girls have boobs the natural way, if you know what I mean. Sure, some say they do, but it's a load of crap. Look at me. I'd be flat as a pancake without a bit of help.'

'Here we go,' said the bra lady. 'Why don't you go and try them on and your mum and I will wait out here.'

I stood alone in the cubicle and all I could see was the white blob of my body, surrounded by mirrors reflecting it back at me from all angles, front and back. I thought my hair was cute. Straight, dark and cut into a pageboy bob. And my face was okay except for all the zits. But the rest of me? Round and getting rounder. Like one of those Valentine's Day cherubs. And not in a good way.

'How are you going in there?' the bra lady asked. 'Sing out if you need a hand!'

'I'm okay,' I said loudly, trying to sound as positive as possible.

'She definitely shouldn't be wearing underwire at the moment,' I heard the bra lady tell my mother. 'You've got to let the breasts fully develop before you move onto anything like that. At her age they change so quickly.'

I knew the moment would come. When the bra lady would want to enter the change room and check the fit. The only thing that made it bearable was the fact that she had even more ginormous boobs than me. If she were all skinny and perfect like Mum I couldn't have coped when she entered the change room and put her fingers under the elastic to see if it was too tight.

'This looks lovely on you,' the bra lady said. 'I love this print. It's gorgeous. I would definitely get this one. You can wear it under your clothes and it will feel more like a singlet than a bra, but it offers quite good support. Just stunning.'

I thought stunning was pushing it a little, but at least she wasn't going on about my puppy fat anymore.

'Let's try the others.'

I felt like I would never get out of there. Trapped on a bra-trying conveyer belt of elastic flicking, boob-examining humiliation. I tried on bra after bra after bra. When I finished with the first pile the bra lady brought in more. And if there's one thing my mum loves, it's shopping. She was super excited when we left with five wire-free styles in bubble gum colours and pretty lace and butterfly prints.

'My little girl's growing up,' Mum said, putting her arm around me. 'You'll be bringing home boys in no time.'

'Winter!' Melody interrupted. 'Are you all right?'

'Yeah, sorry. I was just thinking about Mum.'

'What's she done this time?'

'Oh, nothing. I was just thinking about the time she brought me here to get my first bra. It was ages ago.'

'You can't let her get to you,' Melody said.

'I know. She's been okay lately, except did I tell you she's trying to get me to try out for some roller derby team? She probably thinks it will make me lose weight.'

'Argh,' Melody sympathised. 'I can't imagine anything worse. What's with that so-called sport? So violent.'

'Violence is the least of my worries.' I sighed. 'I'll probably fall over and break my arm before anyone has a chance to bash me with their hockey stick or whatever that thing is.'

I waited for reassurance, for Melody to disagree. Instead, I saw the pity in her eyes and we just stood there in silence as I pictured my flabby, unco body lying face down in the middle of the rink while a group of bad-ass roller-derby girls looked at me in horror, no doubt thinking, 'It sucks to be her.'

Chapter 2: Inspired by the Congo

Because his anxiety prevents him from ever being late, George had been waiting for Melody and me for fifteen minutes.

'There you are!' George grinned from his table in the basement of our favourite food arcade.

'You know we're early?' Melody remarked.

'I know, I know,' George said. 'What have you been doing?'

'Just looking at clothes in Myer.' I took a seat. 'Melody tried on leather leggings.'

'Wild.' George laughed. 'Can you make me a pair?'

'What worries me,' Melody said, sitting down next to George, 'is that I'm not sure if you're serious. I mean, what are you wearing?'

If Melody is Natalie Portman, all prim and classic with long straight hair and capsule pieces tastefully pulled together, George is John Waters meets Willy Wonka.

'It's inspired by the Congo.' George flipped the collar of his leopard print blazer. 'Check out the pants.'

George stood up and showed us his two-piece animal print extravaganza.

'I love it,' I said. 'Where's it from?'

'Savers, of course.'

'Wow.' Melody rolled her eyes. 'You are one crazy Asian.'

George's real name is Hien Trang, but when he was little he decided he wanted an English first name and chose George because he was obsessed with this picture book about a naughty dog with the same name. It was either that or Clifford. This is one story George keeps quiet. These days George tells everyone that he named himself after his hero George Romero. Melody and I are sworn to secrecy.

Before I met Melody in Year 8, it was just George and me. We met on our first day of high school. I knew we were going to be friends straightaway, mainly because when I impersonated Jeremy Wade from River Monsters he totally got it.

'Can you see the muscular body on this fish?' George continued. 'What a monster. Look at those teeth!'

All the other kids just stood and stared, but George and I, we couldn't stop talking. At first I had a little crush on him, but he turned out to be one of those boys who has known he's gay ever since he can remember so there was no point even going there. Which was no doubt for the best. I'm not exactly what you'd call a boy magnet. George once said that if we're both still virgins by the time we're twenty-one we can totally do it. The way things are going with my non-existent love life, I might need to take him up on the offer.

'I'm so hungry,' George said. 'Can we get a double serve of Xiao Long Bao?'

My mouth watered at the thought. I had been meaning to sign up for Weight Watchers, where each food is allocated a certain number of points, and you can eat whatever you want as long as you stick within your allocated daily point allowance. Mum went on it last year when she supposedly got too fat to fit into her size 6 jeans. I wouldn't be surprised if she was the skinniest person ever to join the program in Weight Watchers' history. Still, she swore by it and lost the weight in a month.

'Yum,' I replied. 'Let's get some broccoli, too.' Mum loves broccoli. She ate it all the time when she was on Weight Watchers.

George used the touch screen at our table to order, adding pork ribs, the prawn dumplings and sticky rice to our selection.

'I love this place,' he said. 'It never gets old, ordering via computer with minimal waiter interaction.'

'You're so anti-social,' Melody scoffed.

'It's called social anxiety disorder. *Hello.*'

'Hypochondria much?' Melody said.

'Gosh, the food comes quickly,' I said, changing the subject. I filled my small bowl with broccoli and one prawn dumpling. No rice. 'Can you believe we're invited to Liam's party next weekend? What a coup. Seriously, we're up there with the cool kids now.'

'I don't know if I want to go,' Melody said. 'I've got so much work to catch up on and . . .'

'You have to come,' George urged her. 'Come on, Melody. James Lewis will be there and I need backup. I can't go with just Winter.'

'Thanks!'

'I just mean that if James and I hook up I don't want to feel guilty for leaving you on your own.'

'Yeah, come on, Melody. Please,' I begged. 'Everyone will be there and we've never been invited before. Olivia told me that Liam had a party over the summer and his parents' hedge caught on fire and the fire brigade came and everything.'

'Gee, you're really selling it to me,' Melody muttered. 'Okay. I'll come. But only for you guys. I wouldn't do it for anybody else.'

'So, you and James Lewis, huh?' I asked George.

James was in the year above us at school. Elusive and blue-eyed, he always wore a black 70s leather blazer and black jeans.

'Last week I bumped into him in the corridor and I said, "Sorry" and he said, "No problem".'

Melody looked over at George. 'You know you

have told us that story, like, fifty times already.'

'Come on,' I interrupted. 'At least one of us has the possibility of a love life.'

'I suppose you're right,' Melody said. 'God, I'm stuffed. Let's get out of here.'

'Yeah, I'd better go,' George agreed. 'I promised Mum I'd do the grocery shopping today.'

We split the bill and George headed off to the market while Melody decided to spend a couple of hours in the State Library. Seriously, that girl does not know what it means to relax. I was still a bit hungry but I decided to walk home. It wouldn't hurt to burn some extra calories. I stopped off at a fabric shop and found some stretchy vegan leather that I knew would be perfect for Melody's leggings. I then made the hour-long trek back to my house, feeling virtuous and guilt-free.

Chapter 3: When Kids Say Your Mum Is a MILF

Mum likes to say she's a minimalist with edge. She loves neutrals and Danish furniture, with a witty designer lamp or a giant hamburger sculpture by an up-and-coming young artist. Which means our house looks kind of like an art gallery, all clean lines and OCD neatness. Except for my room. That door stays shut when I'm not home. Mum says it's an eyesore.

'What do you think?' Mum asked me as soon as I walked in the door. 'It's finally here!'

For my mother, the new sofa was a massive deal. The Walter Knoll couch, designed by a small group of handsome Austrian men, was Mum's dream seating arrangement and she'd been talking about it non-stop since she ordered it two months ago. And I had to admit, as she lounged on the pale grey wool and leather, in her signature Paper Denim & Cloth cut-offs and relaxed cashmere blend black tank, she did look like a model posing for a catalogue shoot.

'Gorgeous.' I sat down. 'And comfy.'

I could feel Mum looking at me with disapproval. When she and Dad got together and had kids I bet they thought their genes would mix to create some kind of super species. We'd have Mum's looks and Dad's brains. Now Spencer was in LA trying the actor/model thing (last week he auditioned for *Hoochilicious Party Bandits* because, let's face it, he's kind of a himbo). And me? Well, you should know enough about me by now to realise that my parents' home-style genetic engineering needs a bit of fine-tuning. I was the biggest I'd ever been. Even though I was wearing a flattering ox blood-red pencil skirt and my favourite Blondie T-shirt, I knew she was scrutinising my weight.

That's what you get when you have a MILF for a mum.

I was thirteen years old the first time someone called my mum a MILF. She'd just dropped me off at school in the electric blue left-hand drive Mustang that Dad had imported for her from the States. She was wearing a floaty floral-print tank top, denim cut-offs and cowboy boots. Not many kids had a mother who would even attempt to pull off an outfit like that and I could tell everyone was checking her out.

'Good morning, Sienna,' said Felix Anders, a boy I had known since Prep. He was doing his best to be charming, but I thought he looked like a dick with his baggy shorts and old man suit jacket.

'How's it going, Felix?' Mum said. 'Cool jacket.'

Felix watched Mum give me a kiss and get back in the Mustang.

'Your mum's a total MILF.' Felix leered.

His friend Noah laughed. 'That's for sure.'

I didn't know what they were talking about so I just said, 'Shut up,' and walked away. Later on I asked George if he knew what they meant.

'Is it like milk?' George looked genuinely puzzled.

'What are you talking about?'

'You know, how your mum's skin is pretty white and everything. Like milk.'

So at lunchtime we went to the library and googled it.

'Gross,' George cried out. 'I'm not sure you'll want to know.'

'Why? What is it? Is it really bad?'

'Kind of.'

'I don't care. Please tell me, anyway.'

So George read from the screen.

'MILF, an acronym for mother I'd like to . . . you know, it's a colloquial term common in English and generally regarded as vulgar when spelled out. It denotes a sexually attractive female, usually several years older than the person using the term.'

'That's disgusting! Oh gross. Shut it down! Shut it down!'

George and I were laughing so hard that even Jenny, the librarian who is really cool and nice, asked us to quieten down. But the truth is, I felt really shitty. It sucks when everyone talks about how good-looking your mum is, all the while looking at you and thinking, 'What went wrong?'

'I wish I had a normal mum,' I told George on our way back to class.

'So do I!' he replied, shaking his head.

I told Mum all about what Felix said when I got home from school that afternoon.

'Do you know what Felix said about you this morning?' I asked Mum as she was making after-school green smoothies for herself, Spencer and me.

'Oh, God. What?' she asked, adding way too much kale.

'A MILF.'

'Gross!' Spencer declared. 'Why did you tell us that?'

'The little shit,' Mum muttered. 'That is totally inappropriate.'

I wasn't sure what to say, so I stayed quiet.

'Sorry to say this, Spence, you know I love you,' Mum lectured. 'But teenage boys – actually, men in general – can be pretty crass and stupid. They can also be very sexist and objectify women because they feel threatened and insecure. If he says it again, tell him to piss off!'

'I can't say that at school!'

'You know what I mean.' Mum handed me a glass of green slime. 'Drink this. It's amazing. Kate from roller derby gave me the recipe.'

From that day on, green smoothies always made me think of Felix and Noah perving at my mother.

'Dad's working late so it's just you and me for dinner tonight.' Mum was leaning back on one of her new Marimekko cushions. 'I thought I'd just make up a quinoa salad. Is that okay with you?'

'Sure,' I replied. Having been so restrained at lunch I was starving. But I never liked to admit hunger to Mum, so I kept quiet. 'I'm just going to my room for a bit.'

In our art gallery house, my bedroom is a sanctuary. In the corner sits my brand new Janome, a sixteenth birthday present from Mum and Dad. I have piles of vintage fabrics that I've sourced from op shops and three flying toucans on the wall above my bed that George and Melody gave me when I turned fifteen. On my bed is a Mexican Day of the Dead quilt I made when I was twelve and first started getting serious about sewing. It's admittedly a little wonky, but I was so proud of it, my first big project. A string of coloured fairy lights decorate my bed and a hilarious, yet inspiring, poster of Tim Gunn with the slogan, 'Make it work', is posted above my sewing station.

When I sit down at my machine I am transported. No longer am I Winter Mae Jones, fat sixteen-year-old who has never been kissed. Instead I'm Winter Mae, one of the world's most influential fashion designers, thin and stylish and coveted.

In my dreams.

Mostly I am a self-taught sewer, but I do go to a Monday night sewing class at the local neighbourhood house. A South American woman called Maria who is neat, trim and matter-of-fact, runs the class. She proudly wears impeccably-made clothes she made in the 1980s. There is nothing Maria does not know about sewing.

'If you spend on fabric and take your time with construction,' Maria says, 'your work will last you a long, long time.'

There are two women in the class and one sullen girl called Tessa, who is about my age and attends with her mum. The other women are pretty old, at least forty, and are the types Mum would say have 'let themselves go'. Caroline mainly sews for her two Shih tzus, Doris and Darby, and Tessa's mum, Mandy, loves to make quilts with muted floral prints that are kind of depressing. I've been doing Monday night sewing for almost a year and Tessa has been working on the same pair of pale blue, puppy print flannel pyjamas the entire time. Whenever she comes to a new instruction she has to ask Maria what to do, even when it's something like, 'Fold over and press'.

Still, I keep going, mainly because of Maria. She makes me feel like I can do whatever I want, encouraging me to try new projects and techniques. I just finished a 1950s polished cotton party dress with a boned bodice, handpicked zip and the flounciest, twirliest skirt you have ever seen. Maria said it was my best work yet. Even though she is trim and petite, Maria never talks about my lumpy body when she helps take my measurements. To her, they are just numbers that mean nothing more than the road to a perfect fit. Not once has Maria given me *the look*.

In the sanctuary of my room I laid the vegan leather on the polished floorboards, pulled out Melody's standard legging pattern piece and cut it out. Mum likes to eat early as she thinks it's better for the metabolism, but I figured I could finish them before dinner.

Except that I was starving.

Mum has never allowed chocolate in the house. Occasionally she'll come home with a tiny block of organic, raw, sugar-free cacao and we'll have a square or two after dinner, but let's just say that family-sized blocks of Cadbury Dairy Milk have always been strictly forbidden and deemed toxic. Which is why I make sure I have some hidden in my sewing supply cupboard, a place I know Mum would never look.

So I tried to focus on Melody's leggings, but I couldn't stop thinking about the chocolate. My mouth watered and the craving was so strong it was almost physically painful. Dammit. *Of course*. It was 4pm and this happens to me every single day. I tell myself I'll only have a couple of squares, which inevitably becomes one row. Then two, three, four. Shit.

There was no way I could sew Melody's leggings while I felt like this. So I caved and ate half a block of chocolate, which of course made me feel guilty and ashamed by my lack of willpower. My constant failure in the face of fat and sugar. But at least the cravings were gone.

When the leggings were done, Mum knocked on the door to tell me dinner was ready. We sat down together and had a nice quinoa salad, complete with pomegranate seeds and a glass of San Pellegrino.

'Thanks, Mum,' I said, clearing the table. 'That was delicious.' And I wasn't lying. Mum is actually a good cook, even if she is a little stingy when it comes to portion size.

That night Mum downloaded the latest episode of *Grey's Anatomy* and we watched it together, drinking herbal tea while sitting on the new couch.

'Everyone goes on about McDreamy,' she said, 'but I don't miss him at all. That Dr Hunt. Now there's a dish and a half.'

'Mum.' I frowned. 'Please.'

'Oh, Winter,' Mum said. 'One day you'll realise that a woman is never too old for a good celebrity perv. In fact, it's one of life's greatest pleasures.'

My stomach rumbled and I wished Mum would keep her sexy thoughts to herself.

Chapter 4: Smash Face Sienna

'Mum and Dad are working tonight,' George said as we sat at our usual lunch spot eating sandwiches. 'Wanna come over?'

Normally I love Fridays. But I was dreading today like you wouldn't believe. 'I can't, Mum is making me go to that roller derby tryout.'

'Yikes,' Melody said. 'I was hoping for your sake it was just a pipe dream.'

'No such luck,' I said. 'Why are your mum and dad working on a Friday night?'

'They got some big corporate cleaning job. Apparently the pay is great so they didn't want to turn it down,' George told us.

'I think they're inspiring,' Melody said. 'They work so hard and they'd do anything for you.'

George frowned in thought. 'I guess.'

'Can I come over and study?'

'Sure!' George was his usual upbeat self. 'But can we at least have dinner first?'

'Of course. I'll cook!'

'Awesome,' George said. 'I'm totes open to your

famous fish curry. Mum and Dad left me some money, so my shout.'

I felt a little left out, but I was glad Melody was getting out of the house tonight. George and I are the only kids at school who know the truth about how Melody lives. Most kids assume she is the smart, over-achieving child of uptight professionals. Which is exactly what I thought when we got partnered up in Year 8 science class. To tell you the truth, I was intimidated. Melody was all gorgeous and Eurasian and super smart. I'm not saying I'm dumb or anything, but in what world does a chubby, artsy fashion-head end up being BFFs with a genius princess with perfect hair? Well. I guess it's true that life is full of surprises because Melody and I made the coolest paper rocket in the class. We painted her fluoro pink, with a face that included big red lips and ginormous eyelashes. We called her Zelda. Not only did she fly higher than any of the other kids' rockets, but Melody and I laughed our way through the entire project.

Melody started hanging out with George and me after our rocket-building bonding session but it wasn't until Year 9 that we found out where and how she lived. For the first year of our friendship, when George and I spent time with Melody outside of school, it was always at my house or at George's place. My house, being pretty big, was an easy place to be. Mum loves George and Melody. Sometimes I think she likes them more than me. When they come over she gets all excited, making them taste her latest avocado-based, agave-sweetened, chocolate mousse, or her so-called-famous sugar/wheat/dairy free chocolate chip cookies.

'You'll never guess what these brownies are made of!' Mum will exclaim, excitedly presenting us with a plate fresh out of the oven.

'Oooh, something delicious,' George will say. 'They're so moist and fudgy.'

'Black beans!' Mum will shout. 'Can you believe it?'

Instinct told me not to ask Melody too much about her home life, though I can't say I wasn't curious. I suspected she was either embarrassed about her extravagant mansion or her perfectionist parents. But one day during first period, some time in the early stages of Year 9, Melody realised that she'd left her laptop at home and panicked. I was surprised that Charmaine, our history teacher, let the two of us go home to get it. Usually teachers just made kids use a spare school computer if they didn't bring their own.

'Just hurry back, girls,' Charmaine told us kindly. 'No dilly-dallying.'

As we walked to Melody's place I remember being surprised that we weren't heading to the most affluent part of town where all the houses are perfectly renovated, tastefully decorated in heritage colours and intricate wrought iron detailing. Instead, we arrived at a street filled with identical orange brick town houses, their small front yards concreted and some of the outside walls vandalised with crappy graffiti.

Melody walked through the open gate of one of the town houses. 'God, I wish Mum wouldn't just leave these lying around.' Melody picked up a couple of butts and chucked them in the bin. 'It's disgusting.'

'This is where you live?' I asked, obviously confused. *Public housing?*

'Yes,' Melody replied matter-of-factly. 'I guess I'm not the spoilt princess you thought I was.'

'I didn't . . .'

The door opened. A skinny woman with thinning hair dyed fluorescent red and dark bags under her eyes peered out. 'What are you doing home?' she asked, then looking at me, 'who's your friend?'

'This is Winter,' said Melody. 'Winter, my mum, Kylie.'

Kylie had no teeth. She was scary-looking, the type of woman you would never want to sit next to on the tram. She had the scrawny, haunted look of a crazy person or a drug addict.

This was Melody's mum?

'I just came to get my laptop,' Melody told her mum.

She ran inside to get her computer as I stood outside with Kylie.

'She studies non-stop, that girl,' Kylie remarked. 'Always at the library. Nothing like me. I didn't even finish school. Gets her brains from her dad.'

'Let's go.' Laptop in hand, Melody looked relieved but uncomfortable. 'See you, Mum.'

'I probably won't be home tonight,' Kylie told Melody as we walked away. 'I'll see you tomorrow.'

'Okay,' Melody replied, not even turning around.

As we headed back down the street, Melody said, 'I can't trust her with my computer. She'd flog it off given half the chance.'

'Oh,' I replied clumsily.

'So now you know,' Melody said.

I hadn't a clue what to say.

'You still want to be my friend?'

And for the first time ever, Melody looked so vulnerable I could have cried.

'You idiot,' I said, putting my arm around her.

'Can you get your mum to video your roller derby audition?' George asked, laughing. 'I could use the footage in my next short film.'

'Shut *up*,' I groaned, throwing a scrunched-up lunch bag his way.

'Maybe it will be fun,' Melody said helpfully. 'You never know.'

'I doubt it.' My stomach churned at the thought of what was to come. 'I've just got to remind myself: this time tomorrow it will all be over.'

Earlier in the week Mum made me watch *Whip It* in an attempt to inspire me. 'I can just see you whizzing around the ring like a total boss.'

'I'm no Drew Barrymore.' I laughed bitterly.

'Oh honey,' Mum said. 'You don't have to be. You're Winter Mae Jones and once you get those skates on, you'll be rockin' it. I know you will.'

Okay, so Mum's not-so-secret fantasy involved me being some kind of tattooed roller girl champion with an ironically cool nickname like Shirley Temple of Doom or Dora the Destroyer. Mum's roller derby name, for the record, is Smash Face Sienna. It took her forever to come up with it and she was so proud.

I knew I could never be like my mum, but she was really looking forward to this afternoon. When I got home from school she made me what she called a 'power smoothie' and she'd even bought me a pair of leopard print booty shorts, black lace tights and a skull print muscle tank to wear for the try-out. All a size too small. I stood in front of my bedroom mirror and almost cried. Like an over-stuffed sausage, I could see fat rolls oozing from my stomach, my boobs barely contained while my arms stuck out like pale sticks of fatty cheese.

Mum quickly disguised the look of horror on her face.

'Don't worry,' she reassured me. 'Once you move, those clothes will give a bit. And roller derby is the best workout. You'll tone up in no time.'

We drove to the skate rink in the Mustang. People always looked at us when we drove that car and I fantasised about sitting in a nice, normal station wagon with a normal middle-aged mother who deemed hot pants inappropriate for day wear and tattoos only for those who'd experienced life in the big house.

'Are you nervous?' Mum asked.

'Um, yes,' I said. 'I think you've forgotten that I can't even skate.'

'Oh rubbish,' Mum said. 'Your problem, Winter, is that you lack confidence. You've always been this way, just like your dad. Skating is easy. You'll see.'

Confidence is not a quality lacking in my mother. Back in primary school, when she thought I wasn't listening, I heard her talking to one of the other mothers about how easy it is to rock a job interview.

'You just put on some boots and a mini skirt and it's yours,' she'd said.

I was in awe. *Can boots really do that for you?* I wondered. It's true that ever since Spencer and I came along Mum has never actually had a job, but I believed her anyway and so did the other woman.

Mum's roller derby team is called The Salty Dolls. They aren't actually very good and hardly ever win, but they wear sassy fishnet tights and baby pink tutus and lots of black eyeliner. Mum says they're totes channelling Courtney Love from the 90s, which I didn't really get until I googled her and discovered that she was in fact a grunge style icon and extremely cool person when my mum was a teenager. These days she's a bit of a mess, which Mum reckons is a tragedy. 'Life's hard for sensitive, creative people,' Mum likes to say wistfully.

To even begin roller derby training you have to be able to skate at least one lap of the rink without falling over or holding onto the sides. That's what Mum and I were here to do today. I'm not quite sure why she thought I was capable of that. I wasn't going to transform into the roller derby hipster daughter of her dreams just because I was wearing too small shorts that had begun to cut off the circulation in my thighs.

But I tried. I really did.

'Come on, Winter!' Mum yelled encouragingly. 'You can do it!'

Mum's friend Lizzy, whose arms were covered in vintage pin-up girl tattoos almost identical to the ones my mum proudly sported, was going to be heading the teen team and you could tell she wasn't impressed by my lack of skating prowess. With her jet black rockabilly hair and bright red lips, Lizzy was eyeing me sceptically as I held onto the railing, desperate for support, imagining my real self leaving my body behind like an unimportant shell. There I was floating away, leaves on a stream. Free and unburdened, watching in pity that poor booty-shorted, size sixteen teenage girl, standing clumsily and exposed.

But as much as I tried to disassociate, I knew I was going to have to let go of the railing at some point.

One, two, three . . .

Next thing I knew I was gliding across the rink, booty shorts and all. *Wow*, I thought to myself. *Maybe it's easier than I imagined it would be.*

I picked up speed. Mum yelled, 'Whooo! You're killing it out there.'

I was getting a little puffed as I turned to wave at Mum and Lizzy, cocky and in awe of my unexpected innate ability to skate. Was skating going to be my thing after all?

And that's when I fell. Flat on my face. There was blood. Everywhere.

'Shit.' Mum came running over. 'Winter, are you all right?'

My head was spinning, though the blood oozing from my nose was warm and surprisingly comforting.

Lizzy wrapped an icepack in a towel and told me to hold it against my nose.

'That was one shit-hot fall,' she said, seemingly impressed.

I looked at the curvy, bikini-clad bombshell tattooed on Mum's arm and wondered how it was possible for a daughter to turn out the complete opposite of her mother.

'You'll be right. It doesn't look like anything's broken,' Lizzy said.

'And we would know,' Mum said. 'Players break their noses all the time.'

'Then why would you want to do it?' I asked.

'Because it's totally bad ass,' Lizzy said in her best teen speak. 'Roller derby rocks.'

'I think I just want to go home.' I looked at Mum. 'I feel kind of dizzy.'

'Sorry,' Mum said to Lizzy.

'Don't sweat it,' Lizzy said. 'And Winter, if you ever want to come back, you're always welcome here.'

Mum was pretty quiet on the way home. Poor Mum. I knew I'd let her down.

'You know, we'll have to practise a bit more before you try out again,' Mum said just before we arrived home. 'I guess I forgot that knowing how to skate doesn't come automatically.'

I wanted to scream at her. I wanted to say, 'Look at me! I almost broke my nose and there was blood everywhere. I'm fat and I'm uncoordinated! I don't want to be a roller derby girl. I AM NOT YOU!'

But I just mumbled, 'Okay,' and kept looking out the window of the Mustang.

Chapter 5: Never Been Kissed

After the trauma that was roller derby, I planned to spend the entire weekend locked away in my bedroom sewing. My idea was to use the pictures I'd taken of the blue lace dress to draft a pattern and make a dress that actually fitted me, for Liam's party next weekend. I decided to use a midnight navy lace in the hope that it would make me look a bit skinnier. I wasn't going to lose ten kilos in a week so I had no choice but to fake it. There was something about being invited to Liam's party that made me feel pressured. Maybe I would finally meet a boy.

The sad truth is I'm sixteen years old and I've never been kissed.

Not unless you count the time on Year 6 camp when I kissed Mirko Palovich during a game of truth and dare. There we were, me and these two girls I haven't seen since primary school, Liana and Maggie, asking each other stupid questions like, 'Would you rather kiss Freddy Saunders or stick your head in the toilet?' or 'I dare you to go next door and sing "You Belong with Me" into your hairbrush'. You know, that kind of thing? Maggie in particular had become hard-core boy-crazy all of a sudden and loved recounting the extended pashing sessions she indulged in with this Year 7 boy called Edward. This meant that most of her truths and dares were about boys and sex, things that were still such a mystery to me. I just couldn't imagine kissing a boy. Ever. Or, more like, I didn't think a boy would ever want to kiss me.

'Winter,' Maggie said with a grin on her face. 'I dare you to kiss Mirko Palovich!'

'Get out of town,' I said. 'There's no way!'

Mirko Palovich was a boy unfortunate in both looks and personality. Dumpy and orange-haired, he took pleasure in flicking the bra straps of those who'd self-consciously developed breasts, all the while rating the looks of girls at school out of ten. Sure, there'd been teacher intervention over the years, but no amount of discipline or discussion could stop Mirko Palovich and his demeaning and humiliating treatment of his fellow classmates. Especially the girls.

I should have stuck to my guns and refused, but I don't know, I had something to prove about how fearless I was so I succumbed to Maggie's dare. The very idea of it got us laughing so hard we almost fell off the bed. Even I thought it was funny.

Until the time came to do something about it.

First off, we had to sneak over to the boys' cabin. This wasn't hard. The teachers were hanging out drinking wine or watching TV or whatever it is teachers do to unwind at the end of the day on a school camp they most probably don't want to be at. Of course, it was pretty much impossible to enter the boys' area without them making a lot of noise so I knew I had to be quick. I entered the dorm and saw Mirko right away. He was wearing yellow hamburger print flannelette pyjamas and his orange hair was sticking up all over the place. I held my breath, ran up to Mirko and kissed him right on the lips. It all happened so quickly it's a bit of a blur. But I know for a fact there was laughter and whooping like you wouldn't believe.

I ran from the cabin at a speed that would have made Mum proud. The girls couldn't stop laughing. I was shaking.

'You should have seen his face!' Liana laughed hysterically. 'He couldn't believe his luck, I bet.'

Can I describe the taste of Mirko's mouth? His toothpaste, the bumfluff on his chin? The spots that had started to erupt thanks to the beginnings of a puberty that would no doubt be cruel and unforgiving? I invented these details later on, repulsed and disturbingly fascinated at the same time. But honestly? It was over so quickly I can't even count it as a first kiss. It was just a blip, so fleeting I could almost pretend it never happened at all.

If only.

Mirko went around telling everyone he was kissed

by a 'short, fat dog'. 'She's really into me, man,' he'd say. 'But I'm way out of her league.' No doubt Mirko imagined that he would grow into a serial modelliser, sleeping only with the tall, thin and beautiful. When I think about the whole sorry incident I derive some comfort from the knowledge that Mirko will always lack the charisma and bank balance to ever make modellising a real possibility. But as repulsed as I was by Mirko, I was devastated by his rejection of me. Not only did I feel like a total idiot, humiliated and ashamed; Mirko's reaction simply reinforced what I already feared.

That nobody would want me. Ever. Not even a deadbeat like Mirko.

Boys don't like fat girls.

I knew I really needed to get over the whole Mirko Palovich humiliation. I mean, it was almost five years ago. But sometimes when you're feeling like a fat loser (thanks, roller derby) these memories come back to haunt a person. Which is another reason why I love sewing and making clothes. You need to concentrate on the task at hand. You can't sew a decent straight seam let alone a fiddly zipper if your mind is all over the place. So when Mum and I got home from roller derby, I was looking forward to working on my pattern while listening to Dad's old Joy Division CDs.

Which is exactly what I did until Dad came home.

I'd just figured out how to draft the bodice when I heard the yelling.

'Don't touch me,' I heard Mum scream. 'You stink.'

'It's Friday night,' Dad slurred. 'So I had a few drinks after work. Sue me.'

It was the same old yelling that often happened when Mum and Dad were together. It's been like that ever since I can remember. Nowadays I try to ignore it, but back when I was little and didn't know better I was determined to fix my parents, make them happy. I'd listen to their arguments so carefully that I'd been known to jot down notes in my Smiggle exercise book.

Mum says Dad works too much.

Dad says someone has to pay for all of this.

Mum says it's not about the money, it's about being a family.

Dad says why would I want to be here when all you do is yell and nag.

Once I'd got enough details I'd act all mediator-like, saying such things as, 'Dad, you need to cut back your hours at work' and 'Mum, you need to tell Dad that you love him so that he wants to be here with us'.

Talk about having no clue. The truth is, no one listens to kids. Not really. Even adults who try really hard to treat kids like equals always end up doing whatever they want in the end.

Even so, it didn't matter that my interventions had no impact whatsoever, I never gave up. Until one day I miscalculated. I was probably about ten by then and Mum and Dad were having a particularly angry fight. I heard glasses smashing and plates being broken. I should have known better, but we'd been learning about mindfulness at school and I was planning to tell Mum to take three deep breaths before she decided to throw something. I couldn't have timed it worse if I tried. I'd just entered the room, brazen and filled with ideas of resolution, when a plate whizzed past my father, hitting me right above my left eye.

There was blood and everything and my parents totally freaked out. Mum was crying hysterically, furious and ashamed and saying, 'Sorry, sorry, sorry.'

Dad got all high and mighty and took me out for a gelato, telling Mum that she needed to calm down and think long and hard about what she'd just done. 'Something's got to change, Sienna,' he demanded. 'We've got children.'

Dad and I drove in silence. My head throbbed and I was feeling very sorry for myself. Dad, I could sense, was still agitated; he hadn't yet calmed down from the fight. We went to a little gelato shop we'd been visiting ever since I was old enough to eat ice-cream. It was a kind of safe place, I guess.

'Bella, what happened to your face?' the ice-cream lady asked, concerned.

'Bike accident.' Dad lied so easily, it might as well have been the truth.

Dad let me order a double size, chocolate-dipped

waffle cone and the lady threw in a couple of extra wafers to make me feel better after my 'accident'. I was never usually allowed more than a single cone, and I actually felt pretty sick afterwards. I even remember what flavours I had: chocolate, lemon and watermelon. I don't remember why Spencer wasn't there. Maybe he was at a sleepover or something. I felt pretty special that day, having Dad all to myself, even if it was because my mum accidentally hit me in the head with a plate.

That afternoon, eating ice-cream with my dad, just the two of us, I thought about how great it would be if my parents got divorced. It made so much sense. Why had I even tried to make them love each other when it was pretty obvious it was never going to happen? I had images of Dad and I having ice-cream every Sunday afternoon. On Wednesdays he'd pick me up after school and we'd go to the library and I would help him with the grocery shopping and I'd even learn how to cook. Dad would have to cut back at work, of course, so he'd have time to take care of me properly. It would be so great. Spencer would live with Mum, which made perfect sense and would make both of them very happy. There would be no more fighting and maybe Dad would find a girlfriend and Mum would find a boyfriend and they'd both remarry and I'd be a bridesmaid at both their weddings and I'd end up with barren step-parents who couldn't have children of their own and would therefore be more than happy to adopt me.

I proposed this idea to Mum and Dad that night over dinner. Mum started crying and saying how sorry she was and that she and Dad loved each other very much and that I was never going to be the product of a broken home. Dad said that I didn't have to worry, that grown-ups fought sometimes but that didn't mean they didn't care about each other. The usual stuff that parents say to try to make their kids feel better. Only it didn't work. I didn't feel better. If Mum and Dad weren't willing to get a divorce that meant that nothing was going to change. This was my life and there was nothing I could do about it.

I turned my music up as loud as it would go, but I still heard the door slam and Mum yell, 'Good riddance!'

This wouldn't be the first time that Dad went and stayed in a hotel to 'cool off'. There was a place just around the corner that had 24-hour check-in and cable TV. I followed him there once after a big fight and I begged him to let me stay.

'I can keep you company,' I begged. 'We can watch a movie.'

But Dad refused. Instead he rang Mum, furious, and asked her to come and pick me up.

Like I said before, I know better now. I just stayed in my room and kept on sewing and listening to Joy Division on my laptop, pretending the argument wasn't happening. Besides, it had nothing to do with me.

Mum yelled, 'I'm going for a run!'

I waited until I heard the door slam, then I went straight to the freezer and found Dad's stash of chocolate cookie dough ice-cream. I didn't bother to put it in a bowl. I just grabbed a spoon and ate the entire tub right there at the kitchen counter. Each mouthful felt like heaven. Cold and sweet and gooey. When I finished I took the empty tub across the street and threw it in the neighbour's bin.

Binge Eating 101: carefully dispose of the evidence.

Chapter 6: Curves: The New Skin and Bone

I'd been regretting the ice-cream binge all week but by the time Liam's party came around I was feeling pretty good. It was one of those nights. You know, when autumn is in full swing but the evenings are still kind of mild. Mum and Dad had gone out on one of their post-massive-fight Saturday night dates and my lace dress had worked out just the way I'd hoped. I put on my favourite tomato-red lipstick and squeezed my gut into a pair of Spanx, which I know are not the most comfortable of garments, but they do make you wonder. Where does all the fat actually go?

'Whoa,' George said when I opened the door. 'You look hot!'

'Oh, I'm a bit fat,' I mumbled, looking at the ground.

'Sometimes you really talk shit,' Melody said. 'You are so not fat. I don't know why you always think you are.'

'Yeah,' George agreed. 'Don't you know curves are the new skin and bone?'

'You should put that on a T-shirt,' I said.

We went inside and Melody and George sat on Mum's new designer couch.

'New couch?' Melody asked.

'Yeah. I think Mum got it from Freedom, or maybe it was Ikea,' I lied.

'Comfy.' George lay back against the cushions. He was making me nervous. If anything got spilt on it Mum would seriously have a heart attack and die. The way George was lounging about, you could tell he had no idea that he was sitting on thousands of dollars worth of upholstery.

'Want a drink?'

'Stuff it,' Melody said. 'Why not?'

Mum always makes sure we have a bottle of Snow Queen vodka in the freezer. It's her favourite brand. She loves to tell people it's from Kazakhstan; just the right blend of exotic, edgy and authentic. Mum always drinks it straight so I followed suit and served it straight up.

'Good lord.' George coughed. 'This is strong.'

'You've just got to down it. Like this,' Melody explained, devouring the liquid within seconds.

George and I looked at her in awe.

'It's in the genes,' she said, deadpan.

By the time we left my house we were all pretty drunk. We staggered to Liam's place singing old Nirvana songs.

'Kurt Cobain was so awesome,' George said. 'I wish I lived back then.'

'He was a drug addict who shot himself in the head!' Melody said.

'Mum says it's a travesty that they play Nirvana on Gold 104. She said they even play it at her gym.' I did my best Mum impersonation, which involved waving my hands about in an exaggerated fashion while rolling my eyes up towards the sky. 'Poor Kurt would be rolling in his grave.'

We all laughed.

'Whoa,' George stared up at Liam's house, unsteady on his feet. 'Check this place out!'

Facing Princes Park, it was one of the tastefully renovated double storey terraces that I admired when I walked home from school. It was really beautiful, with a cottage garden and paved path leading to a shiny red front door. Music blared from the backyard and a couple of kids who were sitting on the balcony looked down and waved.

Melody turned to me, her shiny dark hair falling over the shoulders of her new rose print tee. She was wearing the leather leggings I made and she looked like a total rock star.

'I can't believe we're here.' I admit I was kind of awestruck.

'Me neither,' George said, tugging the Rob Zombie tee he'd paired with his leopard print slacks. He hadn't been allowed out all week because of the homemade Mohawk he'd spontaneously decided to give himself. He said that when his dad saw him he looked like he was going to burst with shame and humiliation. 'You'd think I'd murdered the next door neighbour's new puppy,' George said when he told us the story.

'Down the back,' a girl in a white hippy dress yelled from the balcony. 'Everyone's down the back.'

I was feeling buzzy as we walked down the side of the house. A green wall of cascading plants covered the fence, like a scene from *The Secret Garden*. Coloured fairy lights glistened in the courtyard. There were kids everywhere, smoking, drinking, chatting. A couple of girls were dancing to what I think was Tom Waits and a girl with a perfect pixie cut was pashing some guy in black skinny jeans over in the corner.

'I can't believe people are smoking,' Melody scoffed. '*Seriously*. Who does that anymore? I mean, besides my mum.'

'The fashion pack has arrived,' Liam announced as he approached us. 'You all look fab. Glad you could make it. There are some plastic cups on the table over there and I think Stella is bringing out some food. Enjoy.'

Unlike the three of us, Liam is popular and charismatic, the kind of boy who seems older than he actually is, like the twenty-something actors who play teenagers on an array of unrealistic teen soaps I won't name here. He is tall and athletic with curly blond hair and a goofy smile, and twinkly eyes that make everyone fall just a little bit in love with him.

Totally out of my league, of course, but still worthy of a fantasy or two.

'Oh. My. God,' George exclaimed.

'What is it?' I was a little worried, George was almost jumping out of his skin.

'James just made eye contact and waved. What should I *do*?'

'Go and say hi,' Melody commanded. 'Winter and I will be fine.'

George eyed the drinks table. 'I'll just grab another drink.'

Melody tugged his arm. 'Don't,' she said. 'Slurring is not sexy. Trust me.'

Because George almost always takes Melody's advice he courageously approached James. Melody and I sat in the courtyard and drank the champagne we'd noticed in the ice-filled kiddie pool designed to fuel a night of liver smashing, brain cell-crushing underage drinking.

'Cheers,' Melody declared. 'We are not here to impress anyone so let's have fun.'

'Yeah,' I said. 'Stuff it!'

And that's when I spilled my drink all over the crotch of some random stranger who was just trying to find a place to sit down. I don't even know how it happened. But what I do know is that the wet patch on his pale blue jeans made him look like he'd pissed himself.

'Oh, I'm so sorry. It was an accident. I'm sure

I've got some tissues somewhere in here.' I started rummaging through my bag. No luck.

'Don't worry about it,' the wet patch boy's friend said. 'Mind if we join you?'

These boys were a far cry from the skinny-jeaned hipsters that were populating this party. In fact, they were refreshingly geeky and out of place.

'I'm Nick and this is my friend Oliver,' said the dark-haired one with dry jeans and a *Star Wars* tee. 'How do you know Liam?'

'I'm so sorry,' I said to the wet patch boy, aka Oliver, again. He had ginger hair and freckles, but there was something about him that made him cute. His sparkly green eyes, maybe. Or the way he laughed and said, 'You don't have to keep apologising. This happens to me *all* the time.'

Melody nudged me. 'He's funny.'

It turned out the boys knew Liam from taekwondo, which surprised me as Liam didn't seem the martial arts type. Nick and Oliver, on the other hand, were black belt geeks through and through. They told us they went to one of those high achieving all-boys schools, which they both hated but considered academically helpful as Nick aimed to get into medicine, which got Melody all animated and the two of them started talking non-stop, ignoring both Oliver and me.

'So,' I slurred slightly, having no idea what to talk about. 'Taekwondo, huh? I don't really do sports, as you can probably tell – whoa, I love this song, even though I bet they're playing it ironically.'

'People say Flock of Seagulls were one hit wonders, but their whole album is actually pretty good.'

I almost fell off my chair. 'You like Flock of Seagulls? No one likes them . . . well, no one our age, anyway!'

'Don't tell anyone,' Oliver murmured, looking concerned, 'but I have a thing for 80s music.'

'Please tell me you are obsessed with Talking Heads.' I was getting excited. 'I even love their outfits.'

'Totally,' Oliver agreed. 'Though do they trump Devo? That's the question.'

I was just about to get into the pros and cons of each band when I started to feel a little queasy. Okay, very queasy.

'I don't feel so good,' I said. 'I think I drank too much.'

'It's okay. I'll get you some water.' Oliver stumbled away to the kitchen.

If I weren't so humiliated by the fact that I was now vomiting into a pot plant I would have been secretly thrilled that a boy was doing something nice for me. Then I heard the screams. And a crash. And someone yelling, 'Call triple zero!'

Oliver came rushing back with the water. 'Something's happened in the front yard.'

‘What’s going on?’ I grabbed the water and drank it thankfully.

Everyone was rushing through the house, trampling the polished floorboards and Moroccan rugs, to find out what was going on.

‘Oh my God!’ a girl yelled.

‘Hannah! Hannah!’ screamed another.

‘The paramedics are on their way,’ someone said. ‘Don’t move her. They said not to move her.’

A white blob lay in the front yard. It was the white hippy dress girl from the balcony. She was so still she looked dead. Melody came and stood beside me with Nick. Oliver held my hand. The yard was spinning and I felt hot. ‘Sober up, sober up,’ I said to myself, a horrible vomity taste filling my mouth.

‘What happened?’ I asked.

George came rushing over, ashen-faced. ‘James and I were up there with her. There was a bunch of us. She was just mucking around, dancing and stuff, and then she fell off.’

My stomach churned. ‘Will she be okay?’

‘It depends on how she fell,’ Melody said. ‘I think she landed on the garden, which is better than a concrete path.’

The paramedics told us all to get out of their way as they rushed across the lawn toward the girl. ‘Where are your parents?’ asked a young woman, who didn’t look that much older than us. ‘Are there any adults here?’

'They're in the UK,' Liam replied. 'For another week.'

'Is she going to be all right?' someone cried out. 'Please tell us.'

'She's unconscious. The best thing you can do for your friend right now is get out of the way and let us do our job.'

It felt wrong to stick around.

'Let's go home,' Melody said.

'We'll walk with you.' Oliver and Nick looked at us. 'Make sure you get back safely.'

So George left with James and Melody and I walked with the two boys. Nobody knew what to say or how to behave. I felt sick and so tired all I could think about was my bed. When we got to my place I could barely muster up the energy to wave goodbye. I just went up to my room and passed out in my new lace dress, letting my make-up smudge the pillow while Tim Gunn stared down at me all dapper, dignified and disapproving.

Make it work.

Chapter 7: Wake Up

I woke up to a text from Melody.

Have u checked Facebook????

It was filled with pictures of Hannah, the girl with the white hippy dress. There she was in hiking boots on top of a mountain, in a bikini with her good-looking friends on a white sandy beach. Wearing sunglasses and drinking from a coconut. Smiling in her private girls' school uniform.

Wake up soon beautiful girl.

We love you xxxxxxx

Keep fighting. We know you can get through this.

There was a message from one of Hannah's friends telling everyone that Hannah was in a coma and that the doctors weren't able to say when or even if she would wake up.

As you can imagine, her family is distraught. We will keep you updated on Facebook.

I texted Melody back.

It looks bad. What should we do?

What can we do? We don't even know her. It sucks, Melody replied.

My head was pounding and I had a taste in my

mouth that was even worse than last night's vomit. I was wet with sweat and hungry and nauseous at the same time. I needed a shower but it was a risk. I couldn't let Mum see me like this.

I opened my bedroom door as quietly as I could. Mum and Dad were in the kitchen sitting in front of their laptop. They were Skyping Spencer. I had my moment. They didn't even look up as I tiptoed to the bathroom and took a couple of headache tablets. Mum always keeps a packet handy. I've heard Dad tell her off for taking them too often but she totally ignores him.

Spencer, as you know, is my big brother. Three months ago, he and his girlfriend Amanda moved to LA to become actors/models. To tell you the truth, I don't miss him. I mean, Spencer and I have never been close. Not just because he's four years older than me, but he may as well be from another planet. Growing up, all he wanted to do was play sport and be popular. He called me Fatty Boomba when I ran. When Dad was around he told Spencer to shut it when he called me names, but Mum always said it was normal for brothers to torment their sisters. Mum adores him, so as you can imagine, it was a dark day for her when Spencer left.

I wanted to say goodbye to Spencer at home, but Mum insisted we go to the airport in the middle of the night to see my brother off. She wouldn't stop fussing, telling him over and over to check his passport and hotel reservation.

'You don't want to get to LA and have nowhere to go! Can you imagine? My boy lost in that big city?'

'I'm fine, Mum,' Spencer kept repeating. 'Amanda will be with me, remember? We know what we're doing.'

'I know. I'm proud of you, honey.' Mum gave my brother another hug before we hopped into Dad's practical Subaru. Mum tried, trust me, but the Mustang could not hold Spencer's luggage. When I joked that Spencer's suitcase was stuffed silly with his collection of metrosexual beauty products Dad laughed, but Mum scowled and demanded, 'Be supportive, Winter.'

The plan was to meet Amanda and her parents at the airport. I don't know what I was thinking, rocking up in my donut-print pyjamas and Ugg boots. I'd always been intimidated by Amanda, who was confident and arrogant in the way only the willowy and conventionally beautiful know how to pull off. Not that I knew Amanda well. She had only been on the scene for a few months, so their international sojourn was a little controversial to say the least. Mum approved of Amanda's hotness, but if there's one person in this world she loves more than anything, it's Spencer. After he announced his plans to try and forge an international fame-fuelled career I overheard Mum crying to Dad about how it felt like a piece of her heart was being ripped away.

While I'd still rather have been home in bed I was more than a little curious to check out Amanda's family. We'd never seen them before, but I'd heard they were rich and semi-famous in the Melbourne social scene. Spencer said Amanda's mother, aka Marianne St John, was asked to audition for a role in *The Social Landmines of Melbourne* but turned it down. Apparently she is too classy for reality TV. Of course I'd googled her and seen photos, but nobody could be prepared for what appeared before us at Tullamarine airport.

We found them at Gloria Jeans. Surrounded by the discarded takeaway cups and spilt sugar of previous diners, along with a couple of extremely tired-looking families in outfits that rivalled my own, the St Johns were so spectacular they virtually shimmered.

Not that Amanda had to try all that hard. Her hair was up in a messy model-off-duty topknot, highlighting her face that was all big eyes, full lips, a little bit elfin-looking. Had her eyes been a little wider, her chin slightly pointier, she would have looked like a scary cult member. But luckily for her she was perfectly proportioned. Amanda even had the coveted gap between her top front teeth. I couldn't imagine what it would be like to look like that. To have been given that gift, for life to be made so much easier just because of a winning genetic combination. Her father, Max, was what Mum refers to as a 'silver fox', maybe not George Clooney exactly, but I could see Mum blush a little when she shook his hand. But Marianne, she was in another league altogether.

First off, being Persian, she had an accent so exotic it didn't seem real. Her olive skin was virtually unlined, with no obvious signs of Botox or plastic surgery. Her long dark hair flowed and shone like the highest quality crêpe de Chine. She was practically dripping with gold, her long manicured fingers covered in rings. As she stood and walked towards us, smiling a wonderful, not too fake-looking smile, I noticed her shoes. Black pumps. But these were no Nine West designer knock-offs. Mum and I had watched enough *Social Landmines* episodes to know exactly what a red sole means. $800 Christian Louboutin's, that's what.

Dad and I were the odd ones out. There was no doubting that for a second.

Marianne exuded elegant wealth, like Princess Kate or Princess Mary. Mum, on the other hand, preferred a more edgy Kate Moss style. Together they made quite a combination as they talked about how proud they were of their babies who had the courage to go forth and follow their dreams. While Dad talked to Max, I tried to talk to Amanda about her plans for LA. Neither of us was particularly interested, but we made the effort.

'What are you going to do?' I asked. 'It sounds very exciting.'

'Well, we have to get headshots and an agent.

There's a lot to organise. But we know some people and I have a really good feeling about this,' Amanda told me.

You hear stories all the time about people who try to make it in Hollywood and end up teaching Pilates. But there was no self-doubt in Amanda.

'Well, if all else fails, you can always become a Scientologist,' I said.

Amanda sipped her skinny-whatever and turned away, joining in the conversation between the two glamazon mothers. I swear, she never so much as looked at me again.

Me? I just wanted to get out of there.

Unfortunately, we had to stick around drinking coffees and making chitchat. Amanda and Spencer were on the edge of their seats and more than once said something like, 'We really should get going.'

But it was the parents who wouldn't let them leave, until finally they had no choice.

'Mum,' Spencer insisted. 'We'll miss our flight if we don't go through now.'

'Of course,' Mum agreed. 'The time just goes by so fast.'

To give her credit, Mum tried hard to contain herself and when she finally had to hug Spencer goodbye she even cracked a lame joke about him buying her a house next door to a Kardashian when he hit the big time. But on the way home she cried and cried and cried. Nothing Dad or I said made any difference. She was completely shattered in a way I'd never seen before.

'Amanda's family sure are good-looking,' I said, trying to take a light and gossipy angle. 'I mean, seriously. They are straight from a TV series about a really good-looking family who intimidate everyone with their good looks.'

'Is there a show like that?' Dad asked. 'I can't think of one.'

'Maybe we should pitch it and they could be the stars!' I suggested.

'Nobody wants to watch that,' Dad said. 'Too depressing. People only want to hear about losers who make them feel better about themselves.'

'What about the Kardashians?'

'Bunch of weirdos,' Dad said.

But while Dad and I joked around, Mum simply sobbed.

Of course a part of me wondered if she'd feel the same way if I decided to head off to LA to 'make it'. I bet she'd just tell me to go on a diet. 'Everyone in Hollywood is so thin', she'd say.

'Why do you like Spencer so much?' I wanted to ask her. 'Why have you always liked him better than me?'

But I already knew the answer. Spencer was beautiful and I was not.

I heard my phone beep when I got out of the shower.

I picked it up casually, assuming it would be Melody wanting to gossip about the night before and ease her guilt about drinking too much when she had so much study to do AND a possible genetic predisposition to drug and alcohol addiction.

But I was wrong.

Wanna hang out this afternoon? The message from an unknown number said.

My phone beeped again.

This is Oliver, btw. From the party.

My heart started to beat so fast I had to sit down.

Oliver! I knew we'd hit it off because of the whole 80s music connection. Sure, he'd asked me to program my number into his phone, but as my emotional hangover took hold I worried that I had in fact been a slurry drunken bore. And there was the whole vomit-in-a-pot-plant situation. Well. Let's just say that while I was in the shower scrubbing myself with Mum's geranium shower gel I'd accepted the fact that Oliver was just another boy who didn't find me attractive.

I texted back.

OK.

'Oooh, you look nice,' Dad commented when I walked into the kitchen. 'Where are you off to?'

'Nowhere,' I fibbed. 'Just hanging out with some friends.'

'Cute dress,' Mum said. 'Did you make it?'

'Yeah.' It was just a simple floral tea dress I'd designed myself.

'Isn't she talented?' Mum said to Dad, then turned back to me. 'We were just Skyping Spencer. He got a call back for *Hoochilicious Party Bandits*! God, I love that show.'

'Wow,' I said, spooning yoghurt into a bowl. But I was too nervous to eat. I didn't want to stuff this up.

Chapter 8: Does the Dog Park Even Count as a Date?

There are first dates and there are first dates. As in, I had never been on a date before in my whole entire life, but I've watched enough romantic comedies to question whether meeting a boy in a urine-rich dog park even counts.

'I was going to suggest roller skating but I figured it was too nice a day to be indoors,' Oliver said as I approached.

'So I guess I didn't tell you I'm scared of dogs,' I quipped, looking at the giant black mutt of a thing standing beside Oliver. His face dropped. 'I'm just kidding.'

'Well then, meet Bruce.'

I gave Bruce a pat and he slobbered all over my hand. I laughed and pretended that I wasn't totally grossed out and paranoid about contracting tapeworm.

'He likes you,' Oliver said. 'And he's been known to bite.'

I must have looked concerned because Oliver laughed again. 'Just kidding.'

We sat on a grassy hill and watched Bruce sniff other dogs' bums.

'I've just noticed that dogs are really gross. I hope you don't mind being here.' Oliver sounded a little nervous as Bruce licked the privates of some curly-haired designer creation.

'Nah,' I replied. 'We used to have a dog, Penny. But she died last year.'

'That sucks.'

'She was more Mum's dog. One of those small hairless things. She always had to wear a jacket.'

'Oh, a Chinese crested hairless dog?'

'Gee, you know your mutts.'

'I secretly want to be a vet,' Oliver told me. 'But Mum dreams that I'll become the next Steve Jobs, only with a much healthier respect for conventional medicine.'

I laughed so hard I had tears coming out of my eyes.

'Well, I think vets are great,' I said, finally.

Oliver told me that growing up with a single mother has pressures, that he feels he should be grateful for all the sacrifices she'd made. I didn't really know what to say. I couldn't imagine my mum ever being on her own.

'Let's go for a walk,' Oliver said. 'Want to?'

We ended up at the Melbourne cemetery. The sun shone and Oliver and I talked and talked and talked while Bruce ran about sniffing tombstones. I was having such a good time I forgot I was on a semi-date and instead of being nervous, I never wanted the time to end. Oliver was so funny, and he always seemed to get what I was talking about when other people probably would have considered me a weirdo.

'My mum loves Elvis,' I remarked as we stood in front of the Elvis Presley memorial. 'When I was a kid we used to come here on bike rides and once we even left a little teddy bear for him.'

'My mum loves Neil Young. She thinks he's a total dreamboat.'

'Dreamboat! Who says that anymore?'

'My mother.' Oliver smirked.

'And about that crusty old dude?'

'I'm warning you now,' Oliver said. 'That when you meet my mum never, ever refer to Neil Young as a "crusty old dude".'

When.

I looked at Oliver. He was tall, maybe 180 centimetres, and lanky. He was wearing an ancient-looking Iron Maiden T-shirt and tattered jeans. He wasn't super hot or anything but for some reason that made me like him more. I liked how his hair was all messy, like he'd just woken up, and he wore black Doc Marten boots like the ones my parents wore in old photos from before I was even born. I imagined myself kissing him but then Oliver's phone beeped and he checked it straightaway.

'I should head back,' he said eventually. 'My aunty is coming over for dinner.'

'Yeah, me too,' I lied. 'I promised my parents I'd be back for tea.'

I would have stayed out all night if he'd asked me, no matter how much trouble I would have been in with my parents.

'I'll walk you home, though,' Oliver said.

'It's okay. You don't have to.'

'I know, but I want to.'

On the way home I told Oliver all about Spencer and his potential role on *Hoochilicious Party Bandits*. Oliver had never heard of the show so he googled it on his phone and said that Louisa Bandit reminded him of Jackie Collins.

'You know Jackie Collins but you don't know Louisa Bandit?' I teased.

'There's a reason my friends call me Grandma.'

'They don't!'

'Okay, no. But they should!'

I laughed and when we got back to my place we stood awkwardly at the gate while I patted Bruce.

'So I guess I'll see you around,' I said.

'Yeah,' Oliver replied. 'Definitely.'

The light was really beautiful, kind of golden, and the street was quiet as a ghost town.

'Okay, bye.' I stalled.

But after some more awkward shuffling I turned and headed inside. I looked around before opening the door but Oliver was already walking down the street with Bruce.

Chapter 9: Pretty Girls Don't Eat

Pro 'ana' and 'mia' websites

by Winter Mae Jones

- Calories will never fulfil you.
- You can spend every day wishing you had a better body. Or do something about it!
- Before you take a bite remember your priorities. Which would you prefer? A fat and bloated stomach or a lovely thigh gap?
- Nothing tastes as good as skinny feels.
- Skip dinner, wake up thinner.
- Repeat after me: revenge body.
- Fasting tip: spin around until you are dizzy and nauseous. Your cravings will disappear.
- Think like a thin girl. Breathe like a thin girl. Move like a thin girl. Eat like a thin girl. One day you'll be a thin girl.
- Stand naked in front of the mirror as often as possible. Still want that burger and fries?

- Keep calm and stop eating.
- Never reward yourself with food. You're not a dog.
- Pretty girls don't eat.
- Pretty girls don't eat.
- Pretty girls don't eat.

'This is so disturbing,' Melody said, handing the beginnings of my English assignment back to me. 'I mean, seriously. "Revenge body"? Hand me a barf bag right this minute.'

'I know, right? There's stuff like this all over the Internet.'

'What are you talking about?' George asked, joining us at our usual lunchtime spot.

'Sporty.' Melody smirked as she checked out his latest look.

George was wearing a pair of jogging shorts that looked like they were from 1982 with a striped T-shirt and sweatband.

'Vintage activewear.' George twirled around. 'Tada!'

'Nowadays referred to as athleisure,' I said.

'You two are freaks.' Melody rolled her eyes.

'I was just telling Melody about my English research project,' I continued. 'I'm looking at pro "ana" and "mia" websites.'

George looked confused.

'They're basically websites set up by people with eating disorders to inspire other people with eating disorders to become as skinny as possible,' I explained. 'There's all this controversy surrounding them because some people argue that they offer an invaluable support system to those suffering from anorexia and bulimia.'

'What a load of crap,' Melody interjected. 'How is telling people to eat naked in front of the mirror supportive in any way?'

'I guess it's a way to find other people who are going through the same thing as you,' I pointed out.

'Yeah, great,' Melody said. 'How to Vomit Up Your Dinner 101.'

'Yuck,' George said. 'What's so good about being skinny anyway?'

It's easy for George and Melody to be dismissive of people trying to lose weight because they have no idea what it's like to be fat. But I didn't say anything and we spent the rest of lunchtime listening to George recount his first kiss with James for the billionth time.

'It was so romantic,' he reminisced. 'Like a movie.'

I knew I shouldn't be jealous. George was so happy. But still, it was kind of torturous.

'There's no way I'm getting into a relationship until I've got my medical degree,' Melody declared before taking a bite of the sausage roll she'd picked up from the canteen. 'Too distracting.'

'But you'll be old by then!' I said.

'Twenty-five isn't that old,' Melody said.

'Gosh.' George shuddered. 'I'd shrivel up like an old prune if I had to wait that long to get laid.'

'I didn't say I wouldn't have casual sex,' Melody clarified. 'Jeez, you are so old-fashioned. Don't you agree, Winter?'

I failed to reply because I was trying to figure out how many calories I'd consumed that day. Would a banana tip me over the edge? I really needed to start entering everything into my phone.

'Earth to Winter.' Melody waved her hand in front of my face.

'Oh yeah, sorry. If I could get laid I totally would,' I said. 'So long as it wasn't with some smelly old man.'

'For sure,' Melody agreed. 'A girl's got to have standards.'

Chapter 10: There's Nothing Like a Good Style Icon to Cheer Up a Girl

It had been two days since my date with Oliver and I hadn't heard a word. Melody says she can't understand why I don't just text him myself, but George is a little more savvy when it comes to the nuances of dating.

'If Iris doesn't get your mind off that boy, nothing will,' George said, grabbing a handful of popcorn. 'Want some?'

George offered me the bowl but I declined. I hadn't told anyone but I decided to stop snacking between meals and since yesterday I've gone cold turkey on the chocolate. I even gave my stash of Lindt to the family next door, telling them that my friend just came back from Switzerland and brought back way too much and would they like some?

We'd just arrived home from school and even though I had the entire house to myself George and I were hanging out in my room watching a documentary about Iris Apfel, the ninety-five year-old New York style icon with whom we are both obsessed.

My favourite part is when Iris tells the story about a lady from a fancy department store approaching her and saying, 'I've been watching you and you're not pretty, you'll never be pretty, but that doesn't matter. You've got something more important. Style.'

Style.

I get a real kick out of that because in that moment, when I see Iris draped in beads and bangles and turbans twice the size of her own head she looks so awesome that being pretty just seems so, well, *boring* and I think, at least for a little while, that maybe I'm okay. Maybe it doesn't matter that I'm not much to look at, that I can make up for it with the way I dress, with the clothes I know how to make and with the fabrics for which I seem to have a good eye.

'God, my legs are like toothpicks,' George exclaimed, looking at his bare legs stretched across my bed.

'They are so not,' I said. 'You're gorgeous.'

We were sitting side by side. My legs were curled up and I was leaning on George's left shoulder. It felt good being next to him, to be touching a boy, even if it was just George who has been my gay BFF since the cruel and painful beginnings of puberty. After the first time he came over to my house, Mum said to me, 'I suspect that funny little George friend of yours bats for the other team, if you know what I mean. Still, gays make great friends.' And, as it turned out, ever since we met he has, in fact, been a fantastic friend.

'James is on this protein supplement that he swears by. He says it totally makes you grow muscle like you're the Incredible Hulk or something.'

'Eeeewww.'

'You know what I mean,' George said. 'You can't say James hasn't got a hot body.'

'He's okay. But I think you look better. Promise me you will never, EVER, take roids.'

'Oh, all right,' George mumbled. 'I guess I could ask for a refund.'

I wasn't kidding when I told George he was gorgeous. He has shiny black hair that always looks cool no matter how he styles it, his eyes are kind and dark, and for some reason he has never had a problem with teenage acne. He's got cheekbones to die for and I guess he's kind of skinny, but as you can imagine, I don't really get why that bothers him. When he smiles his mouth goes kind of crooked but his whole face lights up so you just know he really means it.

'Oh, I love this bit,' I said just as Iris was about to say something like, 'Well, I suppose it's better to be happy than well dressed.'

'The only thing she's ever said that I disagree with.' George sounded totally serious, but you never know.

I lightly punched him on the arm. 'You're such an idiot.' Some of the popcorn fell out of the bowl and onto my Day of the Dead quilt.

'Now look what you've done,' George grumbled

and we locked eyes and something crazy-weird happened. Instead of looking away we kept staring at each other and I got this urge to kiss him. Like in a sexy way, not in a 'you're my gay BFF way'. And I guess George felt the same, because next thing I knew I could taste the salt on his lips and his mouth tasted like popcorn and Iris was in the background saying that when you get old you have to keep pushing yourself, because all you want to do is sleep. My phone beeped and I ignored it and so did George and we just sat there kissing on my bed.

I don't know why it happened. I mean, I love George, but not in a boyfriend way. Maybe it was because I didn't have Oliver. There was one thing, though, that I knew for sure.

We were going to regret this.

Chapter 11: Let's Act Like Nothing Ever Happened

Mum and Dad have taught me the valuable art of repression: i.e. acting like nothing ever happened. I grew out of the whole 'save my parents' marriage phase' which was followed by the fruitless 'encourage my parents to get a divorce phase'. I am now well and truly immersed in the 'turn a blind eye phase'. For example, nowadays when Mum and Dad have one of their massive shout out loud fights, the next day they organise a date night and walk around the house seemingly oblivious to the fact I obviously heard/witnessed the entire thing. Not once has my mother, a self-confessed over-sharer, ever said, 'Hey, Winter. I'm sorry you had to hear me call your father the c-word. I'm sorry you had to hear him call me an evil, skinny bitch. It must be hard for you, living with two people so clearly embroiled in a dysfunctional relationship'.

No. I keep quiet and so do they.

We just act like nothing ever happened.

Mum's relationship with Grandma Joan is a prime

example of the 'act like nothing ever happened' approach to complicated situations. We don't see much of Grandma Joan. Mum says it was my birth that reinforced the fact that Grandma Joan is a toxic presence in her life. I was a difficult birth and even though Mum really wanted a natural delivery she ended up with an epidural and, finally, a caesarean. She still has the picture of me coming out of her slashed-open stomach, all bloody and screaming. I don't look too happy in that photograph. I'm more like a terrifying devil-spawn from a horror film than a cute little baby. You can even see the bluish grey umbilical cord dangling from my stomach, still stuck to Mum like an alien worm or something. Gross.

'I was quite traumatised after the C-section,' Mum told me. 'I was so, so tired and sore and really washed out. So Grandma Joan walks in and says, "It's just a little cut. Get over it. You should have seen what it was like in my day. Much, much worse".

'Then she looked at you, Winter, and said, "She's just another little human, no big deal". I cried and cried. That's when I realised that Mum is just no good for me. Nothing I do ever means anything to her. She thinks I have it so easy, just because we're not dirt poor. She thinks I'm a lazy housewife with nothing to worry about.'

Mum doesn't talk about Grandma Joan much, but whenever she does you can see her whole body tense up. Grandpa died when I was four. I remember him a little bit. He was a silver fox like Amanda's dad. Handsome in a newsreader kind of way, with hazel eyes that sparkled and a cheeky smile. He gave me a Mars Bar once and told me not to tell anyone, like it was this amazing secret only he and I would share. I did tell Spencer, though, thinking it might make him jealous. He just laughed.

'He said the same thing to me, only it was a Snickers.'

Grandpa was a handsome charmer and Mum says Grandma Joan used to be beautiful, too, 'but once she had me, it was all downhill. She got fat. Really fat. Just like all her sisters back home in Austria'.

These days Grandma Joan is constantly on a diet but her weight always stays the same, even after she ended up with Type 2 diabetes.

So it was kind of weird when I got home from school yesterday and there she was, sitting at our kitchen table drinking a cup of hot, milky tea. I'd spent the entire day trying to avoid George and I wasn't in the mood for chitchat, especially not with Grandma Joan, who made me uncomfortable. But it's not like I had a choice.

'Sit down,' Grandma Joan said when I walked into the kitchen. 'Sienna. Make your daughter a coffee.'

I could see Mum tense up.

'How have you been, Grandma?' I asked.

She had her hair set in a mass of grey curls on the top of her head and she was fatter than ever, wearing some kind of navy kaftan muumuu dress with small yellow roses printed on it. She was the complete opposite of Mum, who was wearing black faux leather leggings and a metallic-grey tank top that draped effortlessly over her super slim torso. On Mum, this looked like a completely appropriate outfit to wear while hanging around the house on a Thursday afternoon.

'I'm all right for an old girl,' Grandma Joan said. 'I was just telling your mother here that I'm selling the house and moving into a retirement village. I'll be joining all the other old fogies.'

'It will be good for you,' Mum said. 'I think you'll really like it.'

'Yeah,' I agreed. 'Don't those places have heaps of activities and cafés?'

'Well,' Grandma Joan replied, 'God's waiting room requires entertainment.'

'*Mum*,' Mum said.

Mum was trying hard to be polite but it was obvious she was struggling. She came and sat at the table with us, her body visibly on edge, her cup of Matcha green tea held firmly. I could tell she was dying for Grandma Joan to leave, but she didn't say anything. When it came to Grandma Joan, Mum was like a totally different person. Meek and kind of downtrodden.

'You're skin and bone, Sienna,' Grandma Joan said. 'What is that horrible drink?' She turned to me. 'Your mother eats like a bird. You'd never know she was as plump as a jam donut until she got to about your age, Winter. Like a cherub she was. Only fatter.'

I looked at Mum.

'I wonder if the same thing will happen to you, Winter,' Grandma Joan continued. 'Though it looks like you've still got plenty of meat on your bones.'

'What did the doctor say about your diabetes?' Mum asked, changing the subject.

'Oh, I check my sugar every day and it's fine. I can't eat sweets you know. And I'm on so much medication.' She stopped to rummage through her old black vinyl handbag, pulling out one of those day-of-the-week pill dispensers that old people seem to love. 'Look at this. Blood pressure, heart, sugar, it's all in here. Dr Grayson tells me I've got too much fat on me but I say to him, "I hardly eat anything. I just retain so much fluid". He's such a nice man. So handsome.'

'Well, as long as you're feeling okay,' Mum said lamely.

I looked down at my thighs, the way they spread out like pizza dough.

'Well I don't want to take up your day.' Grandma Joan struggled to stand. Even though I was feeling super self-conscious about the 'meat on my bones' comment I helped her up as she panted and puffed.

Then she did something very, very odd. She gave Mum a hug and said, 'I love you,' before letting herself out the front door.

Mum stood stunned.

'You know,' Mum said. 'She has never, ever said that to me in my whole entire life.'

'That's strange,' I said. 'For a mum.'

'You don't pick your family,' Mum muttered before telling me she was off to Aunt Maggie's for some more kale and coconut water.

Chapter 12: George Really *Is* Gay

'What the hell is going on with you two?' Melody said. 'You've barely spoken all week.'

'Should we tell her?' George looked at me.

'Look, it's no big deal,' I lied. 'So George and I pashed. *Whatever.*'

'You what!?'

You know how in cartoons a character's eyes literally pop out of their head when something shocks them? Well, that's kind of what Melody looked like just then.

'You're gay!' she said, turning to George. 'We've been listening to you go on about bloody James Lewis like he's Ryan Gosling or something.'

'It was a mistake,' George said. 'No big deal.'

'Yeah,' I agreed.

And I did. Kind of. I knew that what happened with George and me was weird and awkward and ridiculous and that as much as I loved him, I didn't *love* love him. Of course I knew all that. But that didn't mean that when George said that what had happened between us was a mistake, I didn't feel like

I'd been stabbed with a mean and twisted knife of, well, rejection.

A *mistake.* He'd just called me a *mistake.*

'Well, I'm pissed off,' Melody said. 'This could change the whole dynamic of our group. Do I have to choose sides now?'

'No!' George and I said in unison.

'You two had better sort it out, that's all I'm saying,' Melody said before stomping off to see the Year 12 maths teacher who was helping her get the perfect grades she needed to get into medicine.

'What's wrong?' George asked.

'You called me a mistake!'

'No I didn't. I said us kissing was a mistake.'

We sat in silence.

'Wasn't it?' George looked at me quizzically.

'Yes, but still . . .' I couldn't help myself, tears started falling down my cheeks. 'It's because I'm fat, isn't it?'

'What are you talking about?' George put his arm around my shoulders.

'You think I'm fat and ugly.' I was bawling by now. I couldn't help it. Nobody would love me and it was all my fault.

'Winter,' George stated firmly, 'I think you're beautiful, but I'm gay. I've always been gay. I love you but I know for a fact that I will never, ever, be with a woman. Not in that way.'

'I know,' I muttered.

'But if I was, it would be you. For sure.'

'Really?'

'Yes, you idiot!' Then he started singing 'Sorry'.

'Please tell me you are not apologising via Justin Bieber.'

'I know that . . .'

'This is a new low,' I scoffed.

I thought about Oliver. Would he be jealous if he knew about George and me? Or would he not even care?

'Okay, okay. If you promise to stop singing I'll forgive you.'

George grinned.

'Wanna wag the last two periods and go check out Savers?' George asked. 'I need a break.'

'Me too,' I said. 'Let's go.'

Chapter 13: The Phone Call

'Where are you?'

I knew it wasn't good as soon as I looked at my phone and saw that the caller was my dad. He never called.

'I rang the school and they couldn't find you.'

'Oh, I decided to head to the library for a study break,' I lied. But Dad was too preoccupied to care.

'Wherever you are you've got to come home,' Dad said. 'Right now.'

'What's going on?'

I could hear my heartbeat, loud and anxious. There was a time, a few years ago, when Dad lost his job. It was a really big deal for our family. Eavesdropping on my parents' conversation when they thought I was asleep told me that they were seriously panicking about what to do. Dad's mega-wage was what kept our family afloat and his job was everything to him. My parents tried to play it down, of course, telling Spencer and me that it was nothing to worry about and that it was easy for people like my dad to find work because of his skills and connections. But my brother and I both knew the truth.

Mum and Dad were packing it.

Even so, it's not like I got pulled out of school on the day it happened. I just came home one day and found my dad pale and shaky. I'd never seen him like that before. In fact, I couldn't remember the last time I'd seen him home at four in the afternoon. Mum was comforting him and there was an air of shock and bewilderment, a lack of confidence that doesn't usually reside amongst Mum's witty designer pieces.

'I don't want to get into it over the phone. Just come home now. Please, Winter.'

I began to feel panicked. Something bad had happened. 'Is it Mum?'

'No. She's fine. Just get here as soon as you can.'

'Okay.'

I found George looking at men's jackets, rows and rows of rejected pieces that had found their way to Savers. It always made me sad, the way clothing was so easily discarded and disposable.

'What do you think of this?' George asked, holding up a suede bomber jacket, complete with fringing.

'Hideous,' I replied.

'Perfect.' George grinned. 'Come to me, baby.'

When I didn't laugh he said, 'What's wrong?'

'I've gotta go. Dad just called. Something's up.'

'Want me to come with you?'

'No, I'll be fine. I'll text you later.'

'Winter,' George said. Then he gave me a hug, right there in the middle of all those smelly old jackets. 'Whatever it is, it will be all right.'

Chapter 14: A Normal Loving Family

Mum and Dad were sitting at the kitchen table, looking kind of shell-shocked.

'Did something happen to Spencer?' I asked, immediately worried that he'd overdosed on some hip – yet dangerous – party drug, or ended up in jail for indecent exposure during one of his under-the-influence nights out in LA.

'No,' Mum said, her eyes red, her make-up uncharacteristically smudged.

'What's going on then?' I asked, starting to feel very nervous.

'It's your Grandma Joan,' Dad said. 'I don't really know how to say this.' He looked shocked and sickly.

'Is it bad?'

'She's dead.'

'She said she was moving to a retirement village and she was fine.'

I wasn't sure how I felt or how I was supposed to feel. I barely knew Grandma Joan. All I really knew about her was that she was rude and offensive and that she always made Mum stressed out and miserable. She was my grandma, but I wasn't sure

I loved her. Mostly what I felt was guilt. I should have made more of an effort last time she was here. I should have asked her about Mum and why she treated her the way she did. I should have told her that she shouldn't insult our weight all the time and then maybe she would have said sorry, that she loved us and wanted to be in our lives. Maybe she would have known the right thing to say. Or maybe she wouldn't.

Now I would never know.

'We think you're old enough to know the truth,' Mum said. 'My mother, Grandma Joan, committed suicide.'

'What?' I was confused. Did old people do that? Why would Grandma Joan do something like that?

'You saw her, Mum. She didn't seem sad to me.'

All I could think about was how she did it. And why. It was as though, if I understood the way she chose to die, this whole situation wouldn't seem so bad. So creepy. I imagined Grandma Joan, sitting alone in one of her floral print muumuus, making the decision that there was no point in staying alive any longer. Maybe if she'd had a more loving family she wouldn't be dead. Was it our fault?

'She was very sick,' Dad said. 'We didn't know, but she had pancreatic cancer and it was aggressive. She probably didn't have more than six weeks left to live.'

'Then why did she tell us she was moving to that retirement village?'

I was getting angry and shouting. I couldn't help it. Mum started crying harder.

'Winter.' Dad did his best to stay calm. 'This is a very hard situation for all of us.'

'It's okay.' Mum sighed. 'I'm angry too. She must have come here to say goodbye. That's exactly what she's like. Her final passive-aggressive act and now we're all left behind feeling angry and guilty and horrible because we didn't know she was sick and we didn't help her.'

'We couldn't help her,' Dad stated. 'How could we have known?'

Shaking, I sat down at the table. Grandma Joan had killed herself. The last time I spoke to her she knew exactly what was going to happen. That I'd never speak to her again. She was probably planning it all out in her head, figuring out the most efficient way to end her life. Maybe she'd even done some research online; she was proud of her ability to navigate the Internet like a teenager. And yet, she acted like everything was completely normal. Like she'd come to visit out of the blue because she realised she didn't see us enough and she wanted to get to know her family again. Like she wanted us to be a normal loving family.

Yeah, right.

'How did she do it?' I couldn't help it. I waited for Mum and Dad to yell at me, to tell me not to ask questions like that, to have some respect. But they didn't.

I had never seen Mum looking so beaten down.

'She took some medicine. It would have been painless, I think. She managed to get her hands on some Benozen, which means she would have just drifted off to sleep and never woken up. She knew what she was doing.'

'What's Benozen?'

Mum and Dad looked at each other. 'It's an illegal drug,' Dad said, 'that some people believe should be available to terminally ill patients who want to end their life.'

'It's basically poison,' Mum explained. 'They use it to put down animals. She poisoned herself.'

'But then who found her?' I couldn't help myself. I needed to understand what happened.

'Someone from home help,' Dad said. 'She must have planned it so she wouldn't be left lying there for too long.'

'Oh my God,' Mum cried out. 'I can't believe this is happening.'

Mum has one brother, my Uncle Max, who lives in some compound in Saudi Arabia earning heaps of money doing IT. I've seen photos, of course, and we've met once or twice, but I wouldn't recognise Uncle Max if I saw him walking down the street. Poor Mum, I realised. She didn't have anyone except for us.

Dad held Mum's hand and gave her a kiss on the head. 'It's okay, Sienna.' His voice was reassuring. 'I'll help you. We'll get through this. Won't we, Winter?'

'Yeah, it will be okay, Mum.' I gave her a hug.

There was this time, back in Year 4, when Molly Johnson told me that her mum said my mum was a bitch after they'd worked together in the school canteen. Of course I knew Mum could be pretty mean sometimes. But that didn't matter. I was still furious. My eyes burned with tears and I felt so protective, like I wanted to go right up to Molly's mum and tell her that she was the bitch, not my mum. I continued to hate Molly right through primary school.

This felt a lot like that, only a million times worse. And I couldn't even tell Grandma Joan off. Maybe Mum was right. Maybe this was her revenge for being ignored by us for all those years. If that was the case, then Grandma Joan sure got the last laugh. Or maybe she was just sad, scared and lonely. Maybe she didn't want to tell us she was sick because she didn't trust us to help her. Maybe it was just easier for her to go off and kill herself without bothering any of us with her real troubles.

Chapter 15: Who Needs Chocolate When You Have Praise and Constant External Validation?

It was after Grandma Joan died that my problems really started. Not that they felt like problems. At least not at first. Six weeks after Grandma Joan's funeral I was lapping up so many compliments I might as well have won a Nobel Peace Prize. Seriously. Who needs chocolate when you have praise and constant external validation?

Of course, before the compliments came the brutal reality of Grandma Joan's death. Uncle Max flew in for the funeral and so did Spencer. Amanda couldn't make it because she was auditioning for a modelling gig on the Home Shopping Network. Seeing as she'd never even met Grandma Joan it made sense that she didn't rock up.

We picked Spencer up from the airport the night before the funeral. He wanted to catch a cab but Mum insisted. She couldn't wait for his arrival and as soon as she saw my brother walk towards us at the airport, I could see her shoulders relax and her eyes water with happiness. Even Dad smiled uncontrollably as Spencer sauntered over, bleary-eyed and jet-lagged but hotter than ever thanks to his LA tan and pricey dental work that I knew my parents had financed. On the drive home Spencer answered Mum's questions about life in LA. He showed us pictures on his phone of the tiny apartment he shared with Amanda and told us that he was earning good money as a trainer at an exclusive LA gym. Even though his potential role in *Hoochilicious Party Bandits* didn't seem to be happening he insisted that Louisa Bandit was a lovely person and that there was still a chance he'd get a gig with her in the future.

'Really?' Mum and I exclaimed simultaneously. 'You really think Louisa Bandit is lovely?'

'She's great,' Spencer insisted. 'And hot for her age.'

'Eeewww,' I replied.

'Why do people always say "for her age" about older women? Why can't she just be hot?' Mum said.

''Cos most old people are ugly,' Spencer replied.

I could see Mum tense up but she laughed it off.

'The only way to avoid getting old is to drop dead,' Dad quipped.

We were all quiet after that.

I wanted to talk to Spencer about Grandma Joan, but he wasn't that kind of brother. He didn't like to talk about our family, at least not with me. He was always too busy. But just as I was heading off to bed after brushing my teeth I bumped into him in the hallway. I was wearing my donut-print pyjamas and my hair was pulled back in an unflattering low pony. Spencer looked like he was heading off to a Peter Alexander photo shoot.

'Is everything all right with you, sis?'

I couldn't believe it. Spencer was concerned about how I was coping, living with Mum and Dad alone, after everything that had happened with Grandma Joan.

'I think so. I mean, Grandma Joan was kind of a bitch, but still . . .'

'If you want, I'd be happy to work out with you.'

I looked at him, confused.

'At work we always tell people, "Don't eat your feelings".'

I could feel my face burn with humiliation. Shame.

Spencer kept going. 'I'm not being an asshole. I can't help but notice that you're looking a little puffy and I can help. It's my job.'

'Puffy!' My eyes filled with tears.

Even Spencer, who wasn't what you'd call the brightest crayon in the box, realised he'd gone too far.

'I didn't mean it in a bad way,' he backtracked. 'I'm just so used to everyone in the business being super lean and athletic, you know.'

'Wrong answer!' I yelled before rushing off to the safety of my bedroom.

The worst thing was, I'd actually been feeling okay about my looks. I was planning to wear my midnight blue lace dress to the funeral, knowing it would help me feel confident enough to face the day we were all dreading. And Spencer had gone and ruined everything with one word.

Puffy.

That's when I'd decided I'd had enough. No longer was I going to provide fuel for people like Spencer and Grandma Joan and Mirko Palovich to call me names. I was going to become skinny. Powerful. Invincible. I would not get fatter and fatter until I ended up like Grandma Joan, dead in her floral print muumuu and oversized coffin.

It was time I took control.

Chapter 16: Churn and Burn

Grandma Joan's funeral was what you might call a churn and burn kind of affair. I spent the day sucking in my stomach and waiting for the whole thing to be over. Which really wasn't long. It was Grandma Joan's last hurrah, but everyone seemed to be in a hurry to get out of there.

Uncle Max came straight off the plane. He flew in that morning and he was flying back to Saudi Arabia the next day. He looked tired as hell, his face pale and flabby and his gut hanging over the top of his chinos. He had a tan, but that had only aged him further. His skin was like leather. He had Mum's dark eyes, but all her hard work had definitely paid off. She looked at least ten years younger.

'I can't stick around,' Uncle Max said when Mum asked him how long he was planning to stay. 'Too busy at work.' Mum tried hard to hide her disappointment, but I could see it behind her attempt at a neutral face. So could Dad. He put his arm around Mum and said, 'Let's go sit down.'

We moved to the front row, not that seating was in high demand. There were probably only about twenty people here for Grandma Joan, including us. The plan was for her remains to be cremated, her ashes stored at the same memorial park we were at now. A minister, who'd never even met my grandmother, spoke for ten minutes, a condensed and fact-driven account of her life, when she was born, who she married, how many kids she'd popped out. Not once did she mention the fact that Grandma Joan had killed herself.

Mum sat between Dad and Spencer, holding their hands. I sat on the aisle, not sure what to do with my face.

After the ceremony, a sparrow-like woman with short hair, dyed a colour Mum disparagingly referred to as 'menopausal maroon', approached us. She was wearing a black pant suit that made her look like an office worker, but when I looked at her face I could see that her eyes, which wrinkled at the corners, were kinder than most.

'She was at peace when I found her,' the woman told us. 'She knew it was her time to go. She didn't want to die in hospital with a tube down her throat, surrounded by strangers. She was a proud woman.'

'You found her?' I asked.

'Elsie was Mum's nurse,' Mum explained.

I didn't even know Grandma Joan had a nurse.

'That's good,' Spencer remarked. 'I'm glad she didn't suffer.'

'Were you scared?' I asked. 'When you realised what had happened?'

Spencer gave me a look. I'd overstepped. Again. But Elsie didn't seem to mind.

'Oh no,' she said. 'The dead don't scare me, not like the living.' She laughed in a way that sounded like church bells.

'Oh.' I was surprised. 'We didn't know Grandma Joan very well.'

Spencer gave me another look.

'Family's funny like that,' Elsie remarked matter-of-factly. 'You might never see them. You might not even like them, but they're always tied to you, no matter where you are or how much you try to avoid them!'

Elsie chuckled again and even Spencer laughed.

Dad passed around trays of biscuits and after about twenty minutes one of the staff came and told us we had to leave to make way for the next funeral.

It was a relief.

On the way home Mum and Dad talked about how Grandma Joan was able to access such a hard drug and whether Nurse Elsie had anything to do with it.

'We could look into it more, maybe press charges,' Dad said. 'If you want.'

'No,' Mum snapped. 'No way. It's what Mum wanted.'

For once, Spencer and I remained silent.

We were home by lunchtime.

Chapter 17: More Than Just Friend Material

We ordered takeaway the night of Grandma Joan's funeral. I remember it clearly. Thai. I had Tom Yum. No rice, definitely no prawn crackers. Spencer had a green chicken curry. No rice. Mum ate a prawn salad. No rice. Dad ate an entire tub of massaman beef curry with coconut rice and a serve of spring rolls. And a side of roti. Then I went to my room and tried to Skype Melody and George, but I couldn't get through. I wanted chocolate, went to my cupboard and then remembered that I'd given my entire stash to the neighbours. *Phew*. I made myself a T-shirt with some leftover cheap pineapple print jersey (which took 45 minutes, max), put it on and went to sleep. It felt good to be a little bit hungry.

And that's when something shifted. I started to enjoy feeling hungry, empty and light. Okay, so maybe enjoy isn't the right word. But being hungry made me feel kind of powerful, at least in the beginning. I still ate, but I never snacked and I stuck to three small meals a day, with black coffee in between. It was surprisingly easy and no one even noticed, which I guess wasn't that shocking, seeing as Mum had begun to spend even more time at the gym and Dad was always at work and Spencer flew back to LA two days after the funeral. For the first time in my life, I felt like I had some control over my body.

So this is what it feels like to be one of those *girls.*

I also started spending more time with Oliver. I hadn't seen him much since the George-kissing-mistake and Grandma Joan. I missed him. Though, as any girl worth her weight in *The Rules* knows, it's good to act like an extremely busy person while attempting to attract a mate. Like hanging out with a boy-crush is doing *him* a favour. We walked a lot. Me, Oliver and Bruce. We'd meet after dinner and hang out at the dog park, rugged up against the increasingly cold nights, talking and throwing the ball and making up stories about the dogs as if they were people.

'He's a sleazy old bastard, that one,' Oliver would say. 'Look at the way he's eyeing that puppy over there.'

'That one's a reality TV star,' I'd reply, pointing to a perfectly bred 'oodle of some sort. 'She's got a role on *Hoochilicious Party Bandits* with my brother. They'll have a messy one night stand that they'll be too wasted to even remember, only the whole thing will be caught on camera so there will be no denying it. Amanda will dump Spencer's sorry ass and the 'oodle will run off with Ken.'

'Who's Ken?' Oliver would ask.

'Louisa's husband, duh. Don't you know anything?'

'I really like you,' Oliver blurted out.

'Oh,' I muttered like an imbecile, my face red-hot and my heart beating so fast it was like I'd just run a one hundred-metre sprint.

'I mean, you're not like other girls. I can talk to you and you make me laugh, like, all the time.'

I glanced over at Oliver and he was looking at the ground, his cheeks almost as red as his hair. He was a dork, no doubt about that, but he was so adorable it was ridiculous.

We looked at each other, and then laughed again.

'I guess you're okay, too,' I replied.

My walks with Oliver and Bruce were becoming the highlight of my life. My heart would beat a little faster as I walked to our meeting spot at the dog park. I would always wonder, *Will this be the day that he tells me he's in love with me?* And now, it was kind of happening. Okay, so not quite. He might have meant that he just liked me as a friend because of my personality. Maybe I was too fat for him.

So I stuck to my 'diet' and it worked. Pretty quickly, I have to say. Three weeks after I started, I noticed Mum looking at me while I made my green smoothie as a quick before-school breakfast.

'You're looking good,' she said.

Mum had already been to cardio-Pilates class and she resembled a model on the Lululemon website.

'Thanks.' I shrugged like it was no big deal. But it felt pretty great. I was wearing a gold pencil skirt that was usually tight around the hips. Today, it felt loose. My hard work was paying off. Soon, I told myself. Soon Oliver would notice that I could be more than just friend material.

Chapter 18: No Cake, Thanks. I'm on a Diet

The less I ate, the better my life became. At least that's what it felt like in the beginning. I was down to about a 14 when Maria told me about her niece, Mabel.

'She's looking for someone to help her in her shop. Do you know it? It's called Mabel's. She's an independent designer, you know. Very successful. I told her I know the perfect person.'

Tessa was pretending to hem her pyjama pants, but I could tell she was listening in. I was dedicating sewing night to making alterations to some of my favourite pieces as they were all getting too big. My gold pencil skirt was almost falling off me.

'I know you are busy at school, but you'd only have to work Fridays after school and Saturdays,' Maria continued.

'Are you kidding me?' I grinned. 'Yes!'

I didn't tell Maria my main concerns.

1. I'd never had a job before.
2. I was still too fat to even consider a career in fashion.

3. I'd never been much of a fake-it-till-you-make-it type.

'Excellent,' Maria said, handing me a hot pink business card. 'Call her.'

Not many people can pull off wearing a bird's nest fascinator, complete with leaves and baby birds.

Mabel could.

She wore a silk shift dress that matched her blue hair, with gold lace-ups and navy nail polish.

She was fat. Fatter than I'd ever been.

Only, somehow, she was beautiful.

'You must be Winter!' Mabel gushed enthusiastically. 'Aunt Maria told me all about you. She thinks you're pretty ace, by the way. You must be a breath of fresh air after all the flannel pyjamas most of her students try to sew up.'

I blushed. Mabel was so cool, she intimidated me. I figured she must be somewhere in her late 20s, though it was hard to tell. She wore hot pink lipstick and actually knew what she was doing when it came to make-up application.

'Yeah, she's really nice,' I mumbled, feeling like a complete idiot.

'I love your outfit,' Mabel gushed again. 'Did you make it?'

'Yeah,' I said, feeling a bit proud of myself. It was a two-piece ensemble in floral sateen with a pencil skirt and slight crop top that made me feel like I was okay-looking.

'Great colours,' Mabel said. 'You look really cute.'

Maybe Mabel could sense my awkwardness because she made a huge effort showing me around her two-room studio/warehouse/shop. The back room was packed with boxes and fabrics and racks of samples.

'I sell a lot online,' Mabel said. 'Especially tights and accessories and things like that, so one of your jobs will be processing orders and organising shipping. It's really important that items get posted ASAP. It's a tough market out there, which means customer service has to be impeccable.'

Mabel spoke to me like a grown-up, not a teenager. She also seemed to trust that I knew what I was doing even though I had never had a job before.

'This is what we use to wrap online orders.'

Mabel had a giant roll of pale green rice paper on a big wooden table. 'Then we wrap the package with twine and tie on one of these paper flowers. I also like to write a little note. You can just write "Enjoy" or something like that.'

Mabel also wanted me to organise fabrics when they came in and unpack stock. A lot of the shop was full of Mabel's own designs, but she also ordered stuff in from outside.

'And now,' Mabel said, 'it's time for tea and cake.'

We headed towards a sunny nook in the corner of Mabel's studio. Mood boards filled with fabric swatches and sketches covered the walls and three dress forms were lined up, wearing mock-ups that

Mabel had been working on. They were all floral dresses; two had full skirts and one was a more fitted sheath-type dress.

'I love that sheath dress,' I said.

'Yeah, it's cute isn't it? I'm thinking of making it up in an emerald green as well. You know, like real jewel tones.'

'That would be brilliant!' I almost forgot my self-consciousness for a second.

'I think you would totally rock it,' Mabel said. 'Yes, I'm definitely going to make you a green one and you can wear it when you start working up front.'

'You mean, in the shop? With customers?'

'Sure, why not?' Mabel said, as though me working in a cool clothing shop was the most natural thing in the world. 'I think the customers would love you. Why? Don't you want to?'

'No, that would be awesome,' I said, trying to act confident and self-assured.

'Take a seat.' Mabel gestured to a painted blue table decorated with a vase of posies. She then pulled out a vintage floral tin filled with a rich-looking chocolate cake. My heart started to race and I could feel my palms getting sweaty.

'Cake?' Mabel asked.

'Oh, I don't really eat that stuff anymore. I'm kind of on a diet.'

'Fair enough.' Mabel smiled. 'I hope you don't mind if I have some.'

We drank tea and Mabel ate cake and told me how she finished her law degree but only lasted about five seconds as a lawyer.

'I hated it,' Mabel said. 'It felt so soulless. It's a cutthroat world, law. And legal aid was just too depressing. Though I admire people who do that.'

I looked at the chocolate cake. Was it normal that I couldn't stop thinking about it?

'I guess I just wanted to do something more creative, so I started this business. I wouldn't say I'm rolling in it, but it's doing okay. Sure you don't want some cake? It's chocolate and Earl Grey.'

I wondered how Mabel did it. How did she look so gorgeous and seem so content even though she would have been a size 18 at least!

'I love baking,' Mabel continued. 'Further down the track I might transform some of this space into a little café or something.'

'When my dad got retrenched from his job he used to bake cakes all the time. I didn't even know he knew how. Mum's hopeless at baking. She only cooks health food. So it did make a nice change.'

'Ha!' Mabel scoffed. 'There's food that's good for your body and there's food that's good for your soul. This cake, for example, is good for the soul.'

'Maybe,' I said, doubtful. I didn't want to disagree with her too strongly.

'I used to be like you. I worked really hard to be as thin as possible. No carbs, no sugar, no fun. And then one day I woke up and thought, *stuff this*. Life is too short to be so neurotic. It's just food, for God's sake! We're lucky to have it. Now I just try and be relaxed about what I eat. I mean, it's not easy sometimes. We live in a thin-centric world – that much is true.'

'I guess,' I muttered, wondering if I could ever be like Mabel. Confident and strong and happy. 'Especially in fashion. In fashion everyone is thin.'

'Not anymore,' Mabel said. 'There are so many bigger girls online looking amazing and talking about body confidence and fashion. You should take a look. It's really inspiring.'

'Sure,' I said, not expecting much.

So Mabel ate her cake and I drank my peppermint tea and we talked about sewing and fashion and body image. Her confidence was almost enough to inspire me to forget dieting and eat cake. But not quite.

Chapter 19: Beauty Fades. Dumb Is Forever

Melody loves Barkly Square, a suburban-style shopping centre with a giant Kmart and two supermarkets and cheapo shops selling homewares and clothes. She says it makes her feel at home because when she was small her mum would take her to Kmart and shoplift packets of stickers and hair accessories for Melody, along with make-up for herself. It was the most fun they ever had together.

We'd both had a long and boring day at school so we decided to head to Barkly Square for an after-school Japanese snack. I ordered sashimi, justifying the snack by promising myself to only eat a salad for dinner, and Melody had crispy chicken rolls.

'Retail is exhausting,' Melody said, talking about the job at Kmart she'd just started. 'And the customers. Don't get me started.'

'Just wait till you're a doctor and you have to look at old people's ingrown toenails.'

'Stop it!' Melody said. 'I'm eating. Besides, paediatricians work with children!'

Which is when a tall blonde woman wearing expensive Rag and Bone booties and a classic blazer approached us.

'Hello,' she said, looking at Melody. 'Sorry to interrupt, but my name's Jane and I work for Hotalious. It's a modelling agency. I just haven't been able to take my eyes off you. I think you've really got something.'

'What type of modelling are you talking about?' I asked, suspicious.

'Here's my card,' Jane said to Melody, ignoring me completely. 'Oh my God. Those cheekbones.'

Melody took the card, speechless.

'Google me,' Jane said. 'You'll see. Don't wait too long.'

Jane sauntered off in the way only a supremely confident and busy person can pull off.

'What the hell was that about?' I said. 'Modelling? You're going to be a doctor!'

For many years I'd held onto the belief that a person was either smart or beautiful. It wasn't fair to be both. I'd also held onto the belief that Judge Judy was right. Eventually, being smart would be the better option, her famous saying 'Beauty fades. Dumb is forever' reassuring me that I'd win out in the end. And yet, there I was. Sitting with my super smart and physically stunning BFF who had basically been told by a complete stranger that she was destined for an international modelling career. And not only did she eat crispy chicken rolls without gaining a single kilo, she was the smartest kid in school.

'Where's your phone?' Melody said. 'Mine's flat. Google Jane Simpson, Hotalious.'

'You're serious?'

'Come on,' Melody said. 'Just take a look.'

I'm not proud of this, but I was secretly hoping Hotalious was going to turn out to be one of those businesses that require young women to get their kit off for $50. Not the kind of place that represents famous runway and editorial models that it turned out to be.

'Whoa,' I said, so jealous I was having a hard time covering it up. 'They're huge. Melody, this is serious.'

Melody grabbed my phone.

'Shit,' she said. 'What if I could put myself through medicine? It would have to be better than working at Kmart.'

'I guess,' I said.

'But there are so many ethical issues. Do I want to perpetuate unobtainable standards of beauty? Do I want to see pictures of myself photoshopped to the point where I'm unrecognisable? Do I want to be part of an industry based entirely on image? I've got a brain! I don't want to be a hypocrite.'

'Slow down,' I said. 'Melody, I am going to put my jealousy aside because you are one of my best friends and you are gorgeous and you could use a break. Why don't you just go and check them out, see what they say? This could be your chance to pay for uni, and don't you think it would be kind of fun getting paid to wear amazing outfits and having your hair and make-up done all the time? You could travel the world.'

Melody looked sceptical. 'I don't know.'

'Come on,' I said. 'Let me live vicariously through your beauty.'

'Oh shut up,' Melody said. 'You're gorgeous.'

'Call her now.'

'Oh, all right, hand me your phone.'

Chapter 20: Melody Deserves a Break

'You look different,' Melody said, eyeing me.

'She's in love!' George pumped the air with his fists.

'Hardly,' I lied. 'We haven't even held hands.'

'No. That's not it.'

'I might have lost a bit of weight,' I said. 'It's nothing, really.'

'Oh yeah,' George said. 'You look good. Not that you didn't before,' he added quickly.

'Did Melody tell you?' I changed the subject. 'Yesterday she got approached by a woman from a modelling agency!'

'You're kidding,' George squealed. 'OMG. That is awesome. Melody's going to be famous!'

I may as well have turned green, I was so jealous.

'It's no big deal.' Melody shrugged.

'What do you mean, it's no big deal? It's huge! You can get rich and pay for university with barely any effort. This is so exciting!' George said.

But Melody looked stony-faced.

'Actually, while we're here there is something I need to tell you guys,' she said seriously. Her hair was tied back in a ponytail and I envied her her perfect cheekbones. I'd been working so hard to lose weight, but it didn't matter how hard I tried, how much I dieted, I'd never look like her. It wasn't fair.

But then I realised Melody had tears in her eyes. And crying wasn't something she did. *Ever*.

'What is it?' George and I asked at the same time.

We were sitting in our usual lunch spot even though it was uncomfortably cold. It was the second-to-last day of term before mid-year break. Melody had been stressing about her maths exam, but it was over now and everyone but her knew she'd be getting a perfect score.

'Mum's going to jail.'

'Shit,' George said.

'What happened?' I knew Melody's mum had been to court a few times, but Melody hadn't said anything about jail being a possibility.

'Turns out she robbed some house with Johnno and one of them left their phone behind.'

'Idiots!' I wanted to laugh, but wasn't sure whether it was appropriate.

'She told me when I got home last night. She's got court today.'

Oliver and I often saw Johnno and Kylie roaming the streets while we walked. I never said anything to Melody, but they always looked agitated, speeding along the footpath, their emaciated frames and greasy hair making them look like typical drug users.

Sometimes Kylie said, 'Hi', sometimes she didn't. Oliver said they looked worse than the homeless people his social worker mother looked after.

'How long do you think they'll give her?' George asked, concerned.

'Six months, maybe. More? I don't know.'

'Shit.'

'You know, I don't care if I never see her again.'

George and I were silent. Kylie was a disaster. There was no denying it. How she gave birth to a person like Melody is a complete and utter mystery.

'You can come and live with us,' George blurted.

'Or me!' I interrupted, perhaps a little possessively.

'Thanks, guys,' Melody said. 'But Cathy already said I can stay with her for as long as I want.'

Cathy was a nurse who looked after Melody when she was a newborn. Melody always said that if it weren't for her, she'd be just like her mum. Pregnant and on drugs and a dropout.

'Thank God for Cathy,' I said.

'Yeah.' Melody tried to smile. 'I'm really lucky.'

'If there's anything we can do . . .' I said before Melody cut me off.

'I'm okay. It's kind of a relief, you know? Now I can live with Cathy and next year I'll be eighteen. I'll never have to see Mum again. I'm going to have a different life.'

'You'll have an amazing life.' I put my arms around Melody's shoulders. 'You can earn money through modelling and go to uni and become a doctor. It's going to be awesome.'

'I don't know about the whole modelling thing . . .'

'Like I said before. I'm so jealous I could die. But you have to do it, Melody. Don't throw away the opportunity to earn some serious money. You need it. At least go and check out Jane and see what she says.'

'Yeah,' said George. 'You're the strongest person we know. You deserve a break.'

'You guys are the best.' Melody sighed, and gave us both a hug.

Chapter 21: Ramping it Up

So I was never going to be a model, but like I said, I'd never received so many compliments as I did when I lost weight. Even the lady at the local milk bar made me blush by telling me I was looking 'hot'. Then one day, about five weeks in, Mum told me how proud she was to see me eating 'healthy' and offered to reward me with a trip to Topshop.

'I know you're an amazing seamstress, but let's buy you some outfits to show off your new figure!' she said, grinning with pride.

The only person who didn't seem to notice was Oliver. We continued to meet up in the evenings and walk Bruce, but not once did he say anything about my new body. I figured it was because I still had plenty of weight left to go.

I just couldn't give up.

So I didn't. Carrot sticks, skinless chicken breast, tuna in spring water. Skim milk, green tea, chilli to boost the metabolism. Never more than five almonds at a time. Forget butter and peanuts and sausages. Lots and lots of water. Two squares of dark, sugar-free chocolate twice a week. As a treat, so I didn't feel *deprived*. I asked Mum to make zucchini noodles instead of pasta for dinner and quinoa porridge was a staple breakfast. And I stuck to it. I really did. I even avoided going out, telling George and Melody that I had the flu, then gastro, then too much homework, too busy with extra shifts at Mabel's. But no matter how strict I was, how much I restricted myself, the weight loss slowed down.

I plateaued.

Thanks to my pro 'ana/mia' English assignment, I already knew that plateaus are a frustrating aspect of the weight loss journey. I also knew that I was constantly hungry, that I didn't have the willpower to push my diet any harder. I was weak and I felt bad about it, but it was hard enough saying 'no' when the less I ate, the more I started noticing how much food surrounded me. All the time. I felt like I was constantly declining offers of chocolate and biscuits and ice-cream. *Seriously.* Have you ever walked through a shopping centre and noticed how much food is available? No matter what time of day. Muffins, sushi, rice paper rolls, lattes, hot chips, protein bars, fair trade chocolate, pizza slices, smoothies. It's overwhelming. No wonder I got fat, I'd say to myself as I walked past yet another café selling homemade brownies. Who eats all this stuff?

People like the old Winter. That's who. But while I was terrified that she'd resurface, her chocolate-loving, cake-eating fat-ass self, I wasn't confident I could remain perfect, not like Mum. I just didn't have the strength of character.

That's when I read about laxatives.

The more I read, the more it made sense. It wasn't like becoming bulimic and making myself vomit. I was just giving myself a little bit of leeway, hopefully breaking the plateau, helping get rid of any extras. I'd try them for a week, and if they made me sick, I'd stop. It was no big deal. I'd just use them to clean myself out. Detox. Give myself a boost.

They'd be my little secret. Like a superhero with hidden powers.

Chapter 22: Who Knew Diarrhoea Could Feel So Empowering?

At first, figuring out how to get my hands on a packet of laxatives was nerve-wracking. Could I just walk into the chemist and take some off the shelf? Would the pharmacist ask me what I wanted them for? I lay in bed one night and made up a whole story about how they were for my mum who was on pain medication and needed them to stop her being constipated. I'd concocted a similar story last year after I read about Retin A being good for both acne and wrinkles. I walked down to the chemist to buy some and told the grumpy woman behind the counter that it was for my mother's wrinkly skin. The lady looked at me quizzically and said my mother needed to go to the doctor and get a prescription.

Turns out laxatives are easier to get than Retin A. You can buy them at Coles. I could have bought twenty packets and no one would have batted an eyelid. There were so many types. Granules, liquid, tablets, dried prune concoctions. I went to a couple of different chemists and bought a few varieties that claimed to be extra strength. My heart pounded every time I approached the counter, but no one said a word. It was almost too easy.

That night, after my sensible dinner of lean steak and salad, I doubled the recommended dose and waited for results.

It didn't take long.

My stomach cramped and out came my insides, splurting all over the toilet and stinking out the entire bathroom.

'It's like a nuclear bomb went off in there!' Dad laughed as I came out of the loo, shaky yet elated.

Mum told him off. 'Andrew, leave your daughter alone. She's obviously not well.' Then she lit one of her handcrafted Fornasetti candles like it was no big deal.

Rather than feel embarrassed, I actually got a kick out of the fact that no one so much as suspected my secret. Mum even felt sorry for me. Sure it hurt and was kind of gross, but once I'd finished my stomach was flatter than it'd ever been. All those weeks of diet and exercise, when all I had to do was take a couple of pills to get instant results. Why didn't everyone do this?

Chapter 23: Fat Is Not a Dirty Word

It was a Saturday morning and I was going to be working out the front of Mabel's shop all day. Even though I was unashamedly proud of my increasingly flat stomach, I wasn't feeling so good.

'You're looking a bit pale,' Mabel said when I entered the office and dumped my bag. 'Cute jumpsuit, though. One of yours?'

'Yeah.' I shrugged. 'I just made it the other day.'

I'd been sewing like crazy. It helped keep my mind off eating, especially when I was alone in my room at night, hungry and thinking about chocolate. But now my back hurt, my shoulders cramped and I was feeling light-headed and weak. I was trying to keep my fluids up, but it's hard to counteract the dehydrating effects of chronic diarrhoea.

'Have you seen these?' Mabel asked, looking up from her laptop. 'Such classics.'

'Whoa,' I stepped back, shocked.

On Mabel's screen was a black and white photo of a row of naked women doing the cancan. And not only were the women completely naked.

They were fat.

Way fatter than I'd ever been. Some of them were fatter than Mabel. They were so fat their stomachs rolled with flab and their boobs sagged and their skin dimpled and their arms flapped. At first I thought they were ugly. All that skin, that excess. That lack of control. But I didn't want to be rude, so I kept looking at the screen, trying to think of something clever to say in response, something Mabel would like to hear. What would she want me to say?

And I guess that's when I realised that was the whole point. The women in the photo, with their mega thighs and their cellulite, didn't give two hoots what I or anyone else thought. You could tell just by looking at them that they were women beyond caring. That they'd made a decision that this is who they were. That their body was just their body, their fat just fat. Nothing more, nothing less. Maybe that's why they were smiling. Or maybe they were just having fun.

Fun.

'I get it,' was all I said.

'I'm so glad.' Mabel smiled. 'These images are inspiring my next collection. In fact, they are partly what inspired me to embrace my fat.'

'Oh,' I replied.

'When I saw these photos for the first time, something clicked. They made me realise that I am who I am and if I'm fat, then that's part of the deal. Nothing more, nothing less.'

'You're not that . . .'

'Come on, Winter. Fat is not an insult. At least, it shouldn't be. Do you know what *is* an insult?'

'Um . . . what?'

'Shame. Living a life being ashamed of who you are. Feeling that you have less worth than someone else because you don't fit into some skinny ideal. That's an insult.'

'I guess,' I said, as my stomach rumbled.

Chapter 24: My First Client

I didn't tell Mabel about the dizziness. Instead I grabbed a long black from the café next door and decided to push through the discomfort, just like a skinny girl would. I thought about those fat naked ladies doing the cancan. I wondered if they'd ever had sex. Had they ever had a boyfriend? Why did they decide to pose for *those* photos?

I was thinking about the fat women when a man walked into the store. We didn't get many men coming through. Occasionally a bored husband or boyfriend would hang around and offer his disinterested opinion, but mostly Mabel's was a women-only domain. So when this tall, bearded hipster type with striking blue eyes and black hair entered the building I thought he might be the courier.

'Hi.' I blushed. 'Do you have a delivery? My boss is out the back.'

He was seriously hot.

The man laughed. 'No. I'm just here to see Mabel.'

Next thing I knew Mabel was out front kissing the hipster like it was no big deal.

'I see you've met Simon,' she said. 'My fiancé.'

'Oh, right. Yeah.'

The two of them ignored me and chatted about what time Mabel was finishing up and then Simon left.

'Cute, huh?' Mabel grinned before heading back to the office.

'Very,' I said.

I made it through the morning, watching customer after customer trying to see herself from behind, scowling at her stomach, wondering if it was okay to wear a sleeveless top considering that her upper arms were fat and untoned. Huge, in fact. *Disgusting.*

'I'm not sure,' they'd say as they stared at their reflection while I watched and thought, honestly, that their arms looked fine and their backside shapely. But it didn't matter what I said. I was just a shop girl and I couldn't be trusted. I was there to sell, to make money, to lie through my teeth that our customers looked beautiful no matter what I actually thought.

But the truth is, no one ever looked as bad as she said she did. *Ever.* When a customer couldn't zip up the back of her dress I'd simply get another size. No big deal. Not to me. But to those women, the women standing in front of the mirror, it mattered. It mattered a lot. Sure, when a garment was too big, it was a source of pride.

'It's huge on me,' they'd say and pronounce this

fact loudly enough for other customers to hear. 'I need to go down a size.'

But if a top was tight, pants stubbornly refusing to close at the waist, you'd see tears. You'd see the shame. A feeling I knew well. But I was different. These women, these women were all okay. Beautiful even. Me? I still had a long way to go.

My stomach rumbled. I knew I needed to eat, but I'd begun to fear feeling full. Feeling full meant getting fat. Feeling empty meant that the compliments would keep on coming, that the weight would keep burning, that I'd continue, as Mum said to me last night, 'to waste away'. That I'd continue, as Mum also said to me last night, 'looking fantastic!'

Mabel came out. 'Go have your lunchbreak. I'll watch the shop for a bit.'

I ordered a Thai chicken salad with extra metabolism-enhancing chilli. Not the same as my magic pills, but I couldn't risk diarrhoea at work.

I felt better having eaten and was in a much nicer mood when, after lunch, a gorgeous woman wearing a mustard frock with a gathered skirt and navy bomber jacket entered the shop. She wore tan leather brogues and a star print scarf casually draped around her neck. Effortless. The kind of look I would have liked to obtain, but knew I could never pull off.

'Hi there,' I said, trying to be friendly, but not overbearing.

Mabel stressed the importance of making customers

feel under no pressure to buy so that they would feel so comfortable they'd actually want to spend money.

'I love what you're wearing,' the woman commented, pointing to my black flamingo print jumpsuit. 'Is it from here?'

'Oh no,' I told her. 'It's just a homemade number.'

'Really?' she asked. 'Are you a designer?'

'Oh yeah, kind of.'

'Do you do custom orders?'

'Um.' Did I? Yes. Why not? 'Sure,' I blurted out.

Next thing I knew I was taking Lisa's measurements and promising to call her in a week with a muslin to try on. When she asked how much it would cost I pulled $150 out of nowhere and she seemed completely fine with that.

I couldn't believe it. I'd just sold one of my own designs like it was no big deal. Like I did it every day. A feat I knew old fat Winter wouldn't have been able to pull off.

I was so excited to tell Mabel about what had happened I ran to the back office grinning like a crazy person.

'She said she was happy to pay $150! Can you believe it?'

Naturally I had an image in my head that involved Mabel jumping up and down with excitement, hugging me and telling me how fantastic I was.

'You're so talented,' she'd cry. 'Congratulations.'

But that's not exactly what happened.

'That's great news for you, Winter,' Mabel said. 'But did she buy anything else?'

'Um, no.'

'What I'm saying is I am paying you to sell my stock so that I can make money and keep this business going. You can't use it as a platform to market your own business at my expense.'

My eyes welled with tears. I'd always hated getting into trouble. How could I have been so stupid?

'I'm sorry. I didn't mean . . .'

'Look, don't worry about it,' Mabel said, still a little pissed off. 'You know now. I should have asked you to wear current stock when you're here. Before you go home tonight try on a couple of things and take them home. Just let me know what you select.'

'Yes! That would be amazing.'

In the end I got the emerald green sheath dress (Mabel's size 10, which is probably more like a small 14 in other stores, but still . . .) and a black and white polka silk shirt dress. I never would have been able to afford clothes like that if I had to pay for them.

At the end of my shift Oliver came to pick me up.

'Are you okay to go out?' He looked concerned. 'You're a bit pale. Are you sick?'

'Just a bit tired. But I'll be fine. It's just the movies.'

'Actually, Mum's gone out. Want to hang at my place and get UberEats and watch a movie on the couch?'

'Sure,' I said, acting as nonchalant as possible. I'd

never been to Oliver's house, never seen his bedroom, his bathroom. I hadn't a clue how he lived, not really. And now I was about to find out.

Chapter 25: Oliver's House

Mum always says that when you see where someone lives, it's like seeing them naked. Just by looking around the room you can tell how much money they have, who they spend their time with, what they read, watch, eat. You can gauge their favourite colours, or whether they even have any. You know straight away if they're a complete slob or serial killer OCD. Are they someone you want to be friends with or does their taste in interiors make you want to run a mile?

Oliver and I walked for fifteen minutes to the 1970s block of flats he lived in with his mum, Anita.

'I think Mum might have a boyfriend,' Oliver said, turning the key in the upstairs flat. 'She's always going out with this guy from work. Richard.'

He opened the door. 'I hope she does,' he continued. 'Have a boyfriend, that is. I feel bad about her being alone sometimes.'

A musky smell of incense and chai tea jumped straight at my chakras before I had time to notice the mirrored wall hangings and orange op-shop couch decorated with more mirrored cushions and throws.

'Want a drink?' Oliver asked. 'We've got mead.'

'You're kidding. Mead?'

'Yes, I am actually. I know this place resembles a chai tent. Mum's a bit of an old hippy.'

'*Really*?'

'Ha ha,' Oliver said. 'Want a cider?'

'Okay.'

Oliver and I sat at the small Laminex kitchen table drinking our cider. Bruce sat at our feet and I felt nervous in a way I never did when we were at the park. I patted his head.

'He really likes you,' Oliver said. 'He's discerning.'

'No he isn't!' I grinned. 'He likes everyone.'

'Well, he loves you.'

I changed the subject, feeling embarrassed again.

'You should see these pictures Mabel is using to inspire her new collection.' I took a sip of my drink. 'They're all of these super-fat naked women doing the cancan and things like that.'

'Yikes,' Oliver said. 'That sounds scary.'

'They're actually really beautiful,' I said. 'Unexpectedly so . . .'

'Sounds like something my mother would be into.'

'Why?'

'Oh, she's always going on about body image and crap. Before she worked with the homeless she worked in an eating disorder clinic.'

'What about your dad?'

Oliver never talked about his father and I didn't

ask because I was worried that Oliver would say he was dead or something and I wouldn't know what to say.

'I never told you, did I? I'm the child of a sperm donor.'

'Seriously?'

'It's not like you can tell by looking at me,' Oliver said. 'It's no big deal.'

'Do you know who your dad is?'

'Nah. He was some tall med student, that's all I know.'

'Don't you want to find out?'

'People ask me that all the time, but honestly, I don't really care. I mean, it's not that I don't care, it's just . . . who is that guy to me? A bit of spoof in a cup.'

'Well, when you put it that way,' I said.

Then all of a sudden, completely out of nowhere, Oliver leant forward and kissed me. I spilt cider down my leg as I moved my drink out of the way. Oliver's chair made a crash as he accidentally knocked it over, making Bruce jump and run from the room.

It was totally awkward.

'Shit,' Oliver said. 'I'm such a dickhead.'

'No, you're not,' I said, forcing myself to look him right in the eye even though I was so embarrassed I could barely speak.

'So you like me?' he asked.

'Isn't it obvious?'

Oliver shrugged. 'Not really. I think you're amazing and I thought, well, I know I'm kind of geeky . . .'

'I've had the biggest crush on you, like forever. But I thought you might think I was, you know . . .' My voice trailed off to a whisper. 'Not very attractive.'

Oliver looked stunned. 'You can't be serious! You're so gorgeous; I was shocked that you wanted to go out with me at all. Then I thought you might have liked me, you know, as a brother type.'

'That's exactly what I thought.'

Oliver's face fell.

'I mean, I thought you might like me as a sister.'

'No way.'

But instead of awkward silence, the next thing I knew we were kissing again and it wasn't like with George. It was intense and spine-tingling and well, incredible, and I just kept thinking to myself, of all the girls in the world Oliver could have picked, he chose me. *Me!*

And then I thought: *Being hungry. It was all worth it.*

Chapter 26: Best Night of my Life: The Aftermath

Call me regressive, but there's nothing quite like the feeling of having an attractive person thinking you're hot to make you feel, well, hot. So when I woke up after my date with Oliver, I was actually feeling a bit confident. Cocky even. Which is why, in a moment of absolute craziness, I decided to go shopping for the holy grail of negative body image-creating, anxiety-inducing legwear.

Jeans.

You see, I haven't worn jeans since primary school. Jeans are unforgiving. There is no getting around the fact that you are fatter than you thought you were when a pair of jeans that looked about the right size when you pulled them off the shelf won't even pull up beyond your calf. I still remember standing trapped within the confines of a well-worn change room as an eight year old, my pastel knickers wedging up my bum as I hopelessly sucked my stomach in so hard I could barely breathe. Trying on jeans made me feel like there wasn't a single pair of denim pants in the entire universe that would do up over my bulging stomach. And if they did happen to fit, I looked short and stumpy. Nothing like the beautiful, long-limbed models who advertised the $300 'investment' jeans that are supposed to be so flattering they change your life.

But when I woke up that Sunday morning the house was empty and peaceful. Dad was out for the day on 'business' and Mum did early morning gym sessions followed by roller derby training or a walk with her friend, Kate, even on Sundays! Mum had been exercising like crazy lately and she was even thinner than usual, with the sinewy look of a Hollywood actress struggling to hide her eating disorder. We hadn't spoken much since Grandma Joan died. It was easier to say nothing than try and have a conversation. Besides, with my clandestine laxative-driven diet and school and Mabel's and Oliver, I just didn't have the energy. I felt like I'd barely seen George and Melody in the last few weeks. Basically, I was exhausted.

But that morning I put on one of Dad's Johnny Cash records and made myself eat a decent, no-carb breakfast of low-fat yoghurt and fruit and headed out to buy supplies for Lisa's jumpsuit and shop for a pair of jeans.

Divine Jeans is an institution of Melbourne's inner-north. On Saturdays queues of skinny-legged hipsters stand on the footpath waiting to get in to the tiny shopfront. The jeans are made on the premises and they only cost $50. All the kids at school wear them, but can you believe I'd never been inside? Or maybe you can believe it. Divine Jeans is nothing like an anonymous department store. It's the kind of place where people notice you, a terrifying combination of a window display parading jeans so skinny I wasn't sure I could get my arm into those legs and a small, intimate environment where it would be impossible to avoid the gaze of shop assistants and customers who probably all weighed less than 50 kilograms.

But that day I decided to try.

First thing I saw upon entry was a bearded man so slender he was perusing the size 8 women's skinnies shelf. As I stood there, surrounded by shelves and shelves of jeans, I could feel my heartbeat quickening, my palms getting all damp and sweaty, beads of liquid dripping between my gapless thighs. I was about to walk out when the shop assistant, white blonde, red-lipped and, yes, skinny, noticed me and said, 'Hi.'

I still wanted to run but I didn't have the guts. 'Hi,' I answered as confidently as I could.

I braced myself for the 'Can I help you with anything?' question, but it never came. The size 8 man wanted to know if they had any green jeans in his size and I became invisible.

This is your chance, I thought to myself. *You can walk out that door and never, ever come back.*

It had taken me at least 45 minutes to walk to

Divine Jeans. I live in North Carlton, in a leafy street filled with renovated terraces and middle class families with enough money to afford them. But Divine Jeans is further north, on gritty, busy Sydney Road, where trams and cars and Halal butchers sit alongside bridal boutiques and Two Dollar shops filled with hideous plastic landfill, as Mum always likes to say. I like it up there. It's comforting and imperfect. Noisy and hectic, but the kind of place where no one really bothers you.

So I didn't walk out. Instead I went to the size 14 shelf, feeling like I was being watched with disgust when, really, I was so inconspicuous I didn't even bother to ask if I could use the change room. I just walked right in, pulled the curtain across and kicked off my shoes.

I could barely pull the red, high-waisted jeans up over my feet.

I stared at my reflection in the mirror, my purple Big W undies looking tatty and unflattering. The fluorescents highlighted the stretch marks around my hips, the dimply skin on my thighs practically screamed *hello*. I was sweating, from both heat and effort, and that familiar feeling of shame began to rise up. I could feel my cheeks burning, disgusted. I thought I would cry.

But I didn't.

Instead, I took three deep breaths and thought, *You're here now. Just do it.*

So I left the change room without even bothering to put my shoes on and headed towards the bigger sizes.

'These were too small,' I told the girl. 'I might try a bigger size.'

'Sure,' she said, like she honestly couldn't give a shit.

There's no way those jeans were only one size too small. So I skipped the sixteen and went straight to the biggest size in the shop. Size 18.

Size EIGHTEEN.

But this time, it was easy to fit my leg through the ankle opening. Not only could I pull up my jeans, I could even zip them up and fasten the top button. These size 18 jeans not only fit, they looked good. High-waisted and slim fit, I looked like a regular girl rocking a pair of cute jeans. Because, in spite of my body image issues, there's one thing I know. You cannot rely on clothing sizes to tell you where you're at, weight-wise. Mabel deliberately makes her sizing measurements smaller than chain stores because she knows it will make her customers feel better about themselves. She doesn't advertise the fact, but she was happy to tell me all about it. And when I sew commercial sewing patterns, I have to grade between about three different sizes so that the garment will fit.

'It's crazy,' Mabel lamented late one Saturday afternoon as we were packing up the store. 'That women get so worked up on a number. Anything above a size 12, and we think we're enormous. So my size 10 is really more like the 14 of most brands. And it moves more stock!'

So it's not like I didn't know that fashion sizing is completely unreliable and inconsistent but it's not easy, accepting the fact that the only jeans in the shop that fit were a size 18 when Mabel's 10 fitted only yesterday. But I still tried on a second pair of black jeans and it was the same thing. The 18s fitted great and looked like a wardrobe staple that would go with everything. I'd just been paid so I decided to buy both.

The jeans shop girl looked at the tag and wrote 'size 18' in her receipt book. I carefully watched her face, searching for signs of contempt or repulsion. Did I gross her out? Did she feel relief that she was nothing like me? If she did, I couldn't tell. She barely bothered to look at my face. She was so cool and 'I don't give a shit about you and your jeans' seeming. Mabel would probably fire me if I provided such unenthusiastic customer service. But I guess Divine Jeans, with their $50 a pop pants, already had enough customers. And I was grateful for it.

On the way home, as though in a trance, I stopped at the French patisserie and bought two vanilla slices. One for me and one for Dad. Considering I had another 45 minute walk ahead of me I figured I would be burning off maybe half a slice. Well, a quarter at least. I mean, all up I'd have done at least one and a half hours of low intensity exercise. That had to count for something.

When I got home I cut a piece of vanilla slice and put it on a saucer, carrying it to the kitchen table with a cup of peppermint tea. I ate slowly, savouring each mouthful, telling myself this was enough, that I only needed a little bit, a treat. But it was over so quickly and I wanted just a little bit more. So I went back to the fridge and cut myself another piece, just a small amount, a sliver. I couldn't stop thinking about that vanilla slice. So smooth and creamy and sweet, I barely had to chew. It slipped right down, even with the crunch of crust at the bottom. I could feel the sugar rush to the surface of my skin and I felt energised and elated.

Like an out-of-body experience I would sit down and eat my small, portion-controlled piece of vanilla slice. Then I'd wait a second or two before getting up to cut another sliver, a piece so modestly proportioned you wouldn't even count it as food. Not really. I repeated the process over and over again until I'd been up and back so many times there was nothing left but a few crumbs and some icing sugar sprinkled in the paper bag. I'd eaten two vanilla slices and if I'd bought more, I could easily have kept going.

As I emerged from my custard-induced trance, the feeling of expansion was like black magic. I could feel my stomach balloon, my bum gain inches, my legs puff up like marshmallows. I ran to my bedroom and pulled the laxatives from inside my sewing cupboard. I swallowed several tablets with a glass of water and did fifty star jumps. Soon enough I was on the toilet, relief flooding through me as I cramped and shat until I felt there was nothing left inside of me.

The sensation of my fat cells deflating filled me with relief.

Chapter 27: Mix Tape

'So, ladies.' George struck a pose. 'Can you believe that out of us three nerds, I'm the first to lose my virginity?'

Melody, who'd been quiet all day, opened her eyes wide and I would have fallen off my chair had I not been sitting on the grass.

'You're kidding!' I screamed. 'With James?'

'Of course. Who else would want to do it with me? Besides you, of course, Winter.'

'Too soon,' I replied. 'Too soon.'

'So what was it like?'

I couldn't imagine letting anybody see me naked. Especially not Oliver. I had stretch marks and cellulite and my left boob was a little bit smaller than the right.

'Awesome,' George stated. 'I'm in love.'

Melody was quiet as George told us that he and James were talking about going to Vietnam over the summer break.

'I'm not sure if my parents will let me, though,' George contemplated. 'And I don't really have any money . . .'

Poor George. He was so excited about his new relationship but Melody and I weren't the most animated audience. I was still feeling a little light-headed and dizzy after last night's purge and Melody, well . . . she seemed distracted.

'What's up with you two?' George asked.

'I think I'm getting the flu,' I lied.

'Yeah,' Melody agreed. 'Maybe that's what's wrong with me, too. And I've got a meeting with Jane tomorrow, she's just come back from Paris fashion week or something. I'm so nervous. What am I supposed to wear?'

'Model off duty,' I replied with authority. 'Skinny jeans, ankle boots. Slouchy blazer. You want to look chic without trying too hard.'

'What about my hair?'

'Topknot. Bit of lip gloss, some mascara. You want to highlight your natural beauty, show that you're a low maintenance, yet exotic, girl-next-door type.'

'Wow,' Melody said. 'Um . . . thanks.'

'No problem.' I tried to act as nonchalant as possible.

Then it was time to go back to class and I spent the afternoon forcing myself to pay attention as Linda, our psychology teacher, talked about Pavlov's dog.

'Winter,' Linda said. 'Are you all right?'

I didn't have any friends who studied psych and I was sitting on my own.

'Winter,' she repeated. 'You're looking a little pale. Maybe you should go home.'

It's not often that a teacher gives you permission to go home, so I didn't argue. Instead I packed up my things and stood, holding the table as a dizzy spell almost toppled me over.

Linda looked concerned. 'Do you need to call your mum or dad?'

'I'm okay,' I told her. 'I think I'm getting the flu. I'll go straight to bed when I get home.'

'All right,' Linda said. 'If you think you can manage.'

The walk home wasn't easy, but I got there. Nobody was home but on the doorstep there was an old pastel pink tape recorder that looked like it was straight from the 80s. Stuck to it was a note quoting Smiths lyrics.

Oliver.

My whole body tingled with excitement. I went inside and sat on my bed and turned on the tape. There was Oliver's voice. 'Hey, Winter. If you're listening to this I guess you've found my tape. I just wanted to say I think you're awesome. I hope you like these tracks. Every song reminds me of you.'

I was smiling so hard, I felt like I was starring in my own real-life romantic comedy.

I lay in bed listening to Oliver's selection of 80s love songs. There was 'I Melt With You' by Modern English. 'Another Girl, Another Planet' by The Only Ones. 'Against all Odds' by Phil Collins, a song we had both admitted to secretly liking. 'Prove My Love' by the Violent Femmes and 'I Wanna Be Your Boyfriend' by the Ramones.

I lay in bed, my face burning with embarrassment, my heart beating with excitement.

It would have been one of the best moments of my life if only I hadn't been feeling so sick.

Chapter 28: Tell it Like it Is

When I woke up it was night-time. I was so thirsty I walked into the kitchen wearing a T-shirt and knickers, my make-up still on and my hair all over the place. I felt like I was going to pass out.

But still, I was so happy about Oliver's tape I never could have predicted what was about to happen next.

'Oh! Winter. You scared the shit out of me.'

Mum was sitting at the kitchen table in the dark, half a chocolate cake and a jar of peanut butter in front of her.

'Sorry, I was just getting a drink.'

'You were fast asleep when I got home from the gym,' she said. 'Are you all right?'

'Yeah, just a tummy bug or something.'

Mum's hair needed a brush and she was wearing old leggings and a tatty grey T-shirt that I think used to be my dad's. There was a smudge of chocolate icing on her top and around her mouth.

'I just had this terrible sugar craving.' Mum laughed nervously. 'Goodness. I haven't eaten a carb since 2001!'

Even though Mum was trying to make a joke out

of it, there was no getting around the fact that this moment in the kitchen was unsettling. Was my mum a binge eater? Or was this just a one-off?

'Mum,' I said. I couldn't meet her eyes. 'Are you okay?'

Mum sighed, exhausted. 'You'd better sit down.'

I wanted to get out of there as quickly as I could. But Mum was trying to reach out and I could see that she had something important to say.

'I know I give you a hard time about your weight,' she said. 'I don't mean to. I mean, I guess I thought I was helping, stopping you from ending up all neurotic like me. I thought that if you always stayed slim you would never have to worry about trying to lose. You wouldn't end up all messed up about your body.'

Was my mother trying to tell me that she had an eating disorder? It was hard to tell. Which made me angry. I started shaking. I had never told Mum how she made me feel. I had never told her that I always felt like I wasn't good enough because I was too fat and ugly to be her daughter. That I thought she was embarrassed by me because I wasn't hot and skinny, with boys desperate to date me. That I had failed her and everyone else in this good-looking family. Did it even matter that Spencer wasn't that smart? He was gorgeous, and to Mum that counted for more than smarts or creativity or funniness.

But that night I told her.

'You're right.' I was getting angry. 'It *is* your fault.'

Mum looked puzzled.

'It's your fault that I feel like I'm fat and not good enough. You should feel bad because you are so obsessed with food and body image and then you passed it all on to me.'

Once I was going I couldn't stop myself.

'All you care about is how you look. You think it's everything. But what about being smart or funny or clever? What about all the things I am good at? You're supposed to love me no matter what and you don't. You should feel bad.'

'Oh, Winter.' Mum sobbed. 'I do love you. I do think you're beautiful.'

'Yeah, right.' I rolled my eyes.

'I'm so proud.'

In that moment I hated her. And I felt sorry for her. And I was so angry I felt like I would blow up. All those years she'd pretended she was some kind of food-saint, someone who never craved junk food and who had willpower made of steel. When really, she was just a closet bulimic, pretending that her perfect figure was all down to roller derby and green smoothies.

'I wish you weren't my mum,' I yelled. 'You're pathetic!'

I stood and walked out. Leaving Mum to sit alone with her peanut butter and crumbs and her tears and her self-pity. I didn't look back because I knew that if I did I would see a person who looked like an old withered-up balloon, deflated and helpless. A person with nothing left but grief.

You probably hate me now. Who would say those things to their mum when her own mother had committed suicide not long ago? And of course I wished straight away that I hadn't said them. I wished I could have told Mum that I loved her and that I understood. But I couldn't help myself. I was just *that* angry. I didn't even know why, not really. I just knew that I was mad and that I'd had enough of feeling that way.

Besides, it was too late. Some things you can never take back, no matter how many times you say you're sorry.

Chapter 29: A Keeper

I made an extra special effort getting ready for work that Saturday morning. I wore the emerald green sheath dress that Mabel gave me to wear at work and I'd paired it with some faux diamond stud earrings that I'd made a point of buying from her shop. I was determined to impress Mabel with my hard work and enthusiasm, making it clear that I had no interest in stealing her thunder.

'You look gorgeous!' she exclaimed, dragging her A-frame onto the footpath. 'I love that colour on you.'

'Thanks,' I mumbled. 'It's a beautiful dress.'

We went inside and I started tidying the racks before opening.

After work on the day of the jumpsuit incident, Mabel encouraged me to try on half her inventory to figure out what I wanted to wear as my work uniform. She didn't seem mad any more, giving me styling advice and telling me what looked good and what didn't. It was fun, but I couldn't shake the feeling that I'd seriously stuffed up.

'I'm sorry,' I told Mabel as I colour-coordinated

a rack of pencil skirts. 'I shouldn't have encouraged that customer to buy my designs instead of yours.'

'Look,' Mabel said. 'I was pissed off, but the truth is, it's cut-throat out there and the fact that you have paying customers when you're, what, sixteen, is amazing. I'm sorry I came down hard on you. Running a business can get pretty stressful.'

'I think you do an awesome job,' I replied, honestly.

'Thanks,' Mabel said. 'I know I haven't told you, but you are doing a really great job. I'm lucky to have you.'

I wasn't sure if it was unprofessional, but I was bursting to tell someone about the mix tape Oliver had given me. So I told Mabel.

'Oooh,' Mabel teased. 'You're in love.'

'Well . . . I'm not sure if it's love.'

'Of course you are. Good lord, if a boy left an old-school mix tape like that on my doorstep I'd be jumping him in a second.'

I blushed.

'You know what I mean.' Mabel laughed. 'Go for it is my advice. He sounds like a keeper. Are you seeing him tonight?'

'Yeah. He's coming over to my place.'

'Wear that dress,' Mabel commanded. 'You look smokin'.'

Chapter 30: You Might Be Dog Ugly, but at Least You're Not Bitter and Twisted

'Sometimes I wish I wasn't the one with the "great personality".'

'What are you talking about?'

A person might not notice it at first, but as I looked at him, sitting in the sunlight in the backyard, I could see that Oliver was totally cute, but in a ginger-haired Ian Curtis kind of way. The type that Japanese girls have the hots for. I know all about Ian Curtis because my dad is a huge Joy Division fan which has turned me into one, too. Mum says they're too depressing, even though she loves Nirvana. Go figure.

'Has anyone ever told you that you totally resemble Ian Curtis?'

'Really?' Oliver looked pleased. 'You think so?'

'Totally.'

'You're changing the subject. What's with the whole personality thing? You do have a great personality. Isn't that good?'

'Sure,' I said. 'If it didn't mean you might be dog ugly, but at least you're not bitter and twisted about it.'

'That's not what it means!' Oliver said. 'Is it?'

'Yes. It's what people say to homely girls.'

'Well, I promise I will never, ever again tell you that you have a great personality. Instead I will say you have great tits.'

'That's more like it. I guess Melody's glamorous new career is making me a bit jelly.'

I told Oliver all about Melody and the fact that she was now going to be the next Gigi Hadid. And that she was spotted at a daggy shopping centre outside Kmart.

'Wow, I didn't think things like that actually happened in real life.'

'Me neither,' I replied.

'You know,' Oliver contemplated, 'Melody is beautiful, but she isn't you. I love you even though you have an awesome personality.'

'You love me?'

'Yes,' Oliver said shyly.

And then we kissed.

'I love you too,' I murmured.

Oliver brushed the hair from my face and kissed me again, tenderly, his hands moving along my body. I flinched. I didn't want him to feel the fat rolls around my stomach.

'Are you okay?' he asked.

I kissed him instead of answering and this time when Oliver's hands went to my breasts, I let him. *So long as I keep my bra on*, I thought, *he won't be able to tell that my boobs are not quite the same size.*

We fooled around for a while, clothes on the entire time, and then I lay in Oliver's arms while he stroked my hair.

'I'm starving,' he said. 'Wanna get UberEats?'

'Okay.'

The only downside to hanging out with Oliver is that he loves to eat so much his friends call him 'The Digestor'. It's easy for him because he's tall and skinny and has no concept of what it means to be fat. I don't think Oliver is even physically capable of gaining weight. The last thing I'd ever want would be for him to find out how messed up my body image insecurities have become, so I pretend to eat like a normal person when we're together, which is not only fattening, but anxiety-inducing to boot.

Mum came home when we were sitting in the kitchen eating burgers. She was wearing a beaded dress from Sass & Bide that made her look like red carpet material. I took a huge bite of my bun as she walked into the room and looked her right in the eye. Mum pretended not to notice.

'Hi there. I'm Sienna, Winter's mum.' Mum smiled quizzically at Oliver.

Then she shook Oliver's hand and, to give her credit, she didn't say anything embarrassing. In fact, she was on her best behaviour and left us alone after making small talk about Oliver's school and where he lives and how he met me.

'She seems nice,' Oliver commented after Mum left the room.

'Looks can be deceiving,' I replied as I secretly counted calories inside my head.

Chapter 31: My Friends Suck

After Oliver left my place at midnight I forced myself not to take any laxatives. It wasn't easy. I could feel that burger sitting in my stomach like a bomb loaded with lard. But I didn't want to ruin the night by ending it with more diarrhoea so I opened up my sketchbook and jotted down some dress design ideas until I fell asleep.

In fact, I managed to get through an entire week of school without purging. When I wanted to eat, I sewed, and most evenings after dinner I walked to the dog park with Oliver and Bruce.

I can do this, I said to myself. *I can stay thin and not keep taking those pills*.

But then Friday night came.

It had been months since George, Melody and I had a movie night and it felt like forever since the three of us had hung out. I missed my friends and I was looking forward to lounging around in George's living room watching zombie movies.

'My parents scored another massive corporate cleaning job,' George told us as we walked in the door of his small, meticulously tidy two-bedroom terrace. 'They're working all weekend and won't be back for ages.'

'Awesome,' said Melody. 'Cathy is amazing but she doesn't go out much. Her friends come over and they play bridge and drink gin. Or she watches Netflix.'

'I've been avoiding my parents for weeks,' I said looking at the ground. 'Ever since Mum and I had that fight we've barely spoken.'

'That sounds stressful,' Melody said.

'I guess,' I said. 'It's okay.'

We took off our shoes and George headed to the kitchen to set up his famous dinosaur-shaped popcorn-making machine. Melody and I turned off the lights in the TV room and got everything ready for the movies.

'I'm so hungry,' George said, carrying in a giant bowl of popcorn. 'Want me to run down the street and get fish and chips?'

'Yes, please!' Melody's stomach actually grumbled. 'I'll have a piece of flake and a couple of potato cakes, thanks.'

'What about you, Winter?' George looked at me expectantly.

'I'm not super hungry.' I was really hungry after my shift at Mabel's, but the mere thought of downing hundreds of empty calories was practically giving me heart palpitations.

'Just get the same as me,' Melody suggested.

'You'll probably feel like eating by the time George gets back.'

George was out the door before I had a chance to protest or make up some lie about turning vegan. As much as I feared gaining weight, there was a part of me that missed being fat, the relief of being able to eat without feeling like every mouthful counted for something. Back when I was fat the damage had already been done, the worst had happened, my stomach bulged and my thighs chafed and sure, I could still get bigger, but once you hit a certain point a kilo or two doesn't pack much of a punch. But when you lose weight all that changes. Gaining weight suddenly feels like the worst thing that can ever happen. Sure, the fat clothes I couldn't be bothered adjusting were sitting lonely in an op-shop somewhere, waiting for another girl like the person I used to be. But I knew I couldn't become complacent, that the old fat Winter could resurface in a matter of weeks. Fish and chips for dinner, a burger with Oliver, a bowl of ice-cream. It wouldn't take long for the weight to creep back on.

'Are you all right?' Melody looked at me with concern. 'You look pale.'

'I'm fine,' I said, working super hard to control my breathing. 'Probably just low blood sugar.'

On cue, George walked through the front door. 'Dinner is served, ladies,' he half-sang in a pretend posh voice.

The fish and chips smelt salty and greasy and delicious. They were a favourite before I declared fried food to be the work of the devil.

'Yum,' I said in my best authentically enthusiastic voice. 'I haven't had fish and chips for ages!'

We ate on the couch. George told us that he and James were having a break from each other this weekend.

'Oh, George!' I was concerned. 'What happened? Why didn't you tell us?'

'Seriously, it's no big deal,' George said. 'You might have noticed how much we've been hanging out lately. We don't want to kill the romance by overdoing it, that's all.'

'Sounds like a good idea to me.' Melody nodded. 'It's important to maintain your own individual identity in a relationship.'

I was too busy stressing about the fish and chips I was shoving into my mouth to think of anything decent to add.

Dieting 101: *avoid trigger foods*. Trigger foods are high calorie, low nutrition meals and snacks that encourage overeating and weight gain. I forgot how much I loved fish and chips. The salty, crispy batter, the oil on my tongue. It was one thing to smell them, but eating them . . .

I felt out of control.

'It's good to see you eating,' Melody said. 'We've been a bit worried about you.'

I was so engrossed in eating, I'd forgotten to hide how much I was enjoying myself.

'What do you mean?'

'Well . . .' Melody chose her words carefully. 'You've been looking kind of *gaunt* lately.'

'And you're so tired,' George chimed in.

'I am not.'

'Yes you are,' Melody insisted. 'We've been worried for a while now. We need to know that you're not doing anything stupid.'

'I'm not an idiot,' I said defensively.

'No one's saying that.' Melody tried to calm me down. 'We care about you and we're worried, that's all.'

'Well, you don't need to be. In fact, it's the opposite. I'm just looking after myself, that's all. And being super healthy. If you really cared, you wouldn't have organised fish and chips tonight.'

I knew I shouldn't have said that, but the words just came out before I could think about what I was saying.

'What are you talking about?' demanded Melody. 'Winter, seriously, eating fish and chips on a Friday night with your friends is normal. It's healthy. It's fun.'

'It's not healthy,' I stated. My heart was racing and my stomach felt full of butterflies. What was happening to me? 'I'm sick of everyone always trying to make me eat junk!'

Melody shot George a *look*.

'We're worried that you might be developing an eating disorder,' Melody said.

'Is that what you've been saying about me?'

'I told you not to say anything tonight,' George hissed at Melody.

'What are we supposed to do?' Melody was getting really angry. 'Just sit back and watch her starve to death?'

'You're not a doctor.' I looked at Melody, furious. 'And you probably never will be now that you're joining that modelling agency.'

I stood up. All I wanted was to get out of there. I had a bellyful of fat and I could already feel myself expanding. Breathe in, breathe out, I told myself. My heart was beginning to race.

George leapt up from his chair. 'What the hell?'

'I just want to go home,' I said.

'Don't be stupid.' George looked frantic. 'We haven't even watched the movie yet. Winter, don't go.'

'Please stay,' Melody pleaded, her eyes filled with tears. 'We can talk.'

With that, I stood up, put my shoes back on, and left. I wanted to throw up I was so angry. They'd been talking about me. Rather than support my success, they were telling me I was crazy and sick. *Stuff that*, I thought. *Stuff them, stuff this. Actually, stuff everything. Bloody hypocrites, the pair of them.*

I walked home as fast as I could, thinking non-stop about all the calories I'd consumed and how my friends were a bunch of weight loss saboteurs. I could feel the oil, the fat, the grease, oozing through my pores like sweat. I was disgusting. Fat. Hideous. Gross.

As soon as I got home I had a cold shower, scrubbing myself with a loofah, trying to stimulate the fat cells to shrivel and die and leave me alone. Of course, I also took a bunch of laxatives. I waited impatiently for my stomach to cramp, to feel empty and light. Why weren't they kicking in? I took some more.

I anticipated the painful stomach cramps like they were something to look forward to. I deserved them. In that moment all I cared about was getting rid of all horrible, fatty food. I barely gave a second thought to my friends and the fact that I'd walked out on them when all they'd tried to do was make sure I was okay.

So there I was on a Friday night, lying in bed after ditching my friends, waiting in anticipation for the diarrhoea to kick in.

All because I wanted to be a size 8.

Chapter 32: Don't Try This at Home

When I woke up in hospital I mostly felt shame. And a little bit of fear. But yeah, shame, most definitely shame. It was really, really embarrassing.

Back in Year 5 there was this kid, Michael Scott. He was in my class but we weren't really friends or anything. He was okay. Just one of those boys who collected footy cards and spent lunchtimes running around playing sport. Then one day our teacher, Zoe, stood in front of the class and said she had some sad news about Michael.

'Michael has leukaemia,' Zoe announced. 'Does anyone know what that means?'

I did. I had watched *My Sister's Keeper* with Mum and Spencer just a month before.

'It means he has cancer,' I replied.

Some of the girls cried, especially Katie who'd been in love with Michael since Prep.

'Is he going to die?' Lenny had asked. He wasn't being mean. He just wanted to know.

'No,' Zoe answered. 'But he is very sick and won't be at school for a while.'

We had a big class discussion about chemotherapy

and cancer and what it means and how your hair falls out and how scary this whole experience must be for Michael and his family. Then we spent the morning making a card and everyone in the class wrote a get well note for Michael, telling him that we were thinking of him and how brave he must be. His best friend Sam delivered the messages after school that day.

'We played Minecraft in his hospital bed,' Sam told the class. 'He's acting really cool. I think he's going to be okay.'

'Hardly any kids die of leukaemia these days,' is what Mum told me when I got home from school. 'Cancer treatment is so much better than it used to be. He'll be okay, I promise.'

It seemed like Mum was right. Michael had chemo and even came back to school. He played football and acted normal. He didn't say much about the hospital and if anyone asked he went kind of quiet and just mumbled a response in as few words as possible. He was nothing like Lilly, this loudmouth kid who was really gross and brought her tonsils to school in a jar after she had them removed. Michael wasn't proud of what he'd been through. I don't know if he was ashamed, exactly, but he didn't like anyone to make a big deal out of it. The last thing he wanted was to be seen as the sick kid.

Michael was still alive at the end of Year 6. He'd had big chunks of time off here and there but I guess we'd all forgotten that death was even a possibility. We just got used to him coming in and out. We were self-absorbed, I guess, all caught up in the drama of heading off to high school.

I didn't think too much about Michael. I mean, in my mind cancer kids were those skinny hairless kids who get paraded around on bad current affairs shows with tear-inducing music in the background. I didn't know anyone like that. Michael always wore a hat until his hair grew back. He never went on about his cancer. It was easy to act like it had never happened.

We went to different high schools and I didn't think about him much until, one afternoon in Year 7, Mum came and interrupted me while I was watching old *Buffy the Vampire Slayer* episodes. I was annoyed with her. Spike and Buffy were about to kiss for the first time.

'I have some very sad news.' Mum looked all bleary-eyed. 'I just found out that that boy from primary school, Michael . . . He died two days ago.'

'No,' I gasped. 'That can't be right. He recovered.'

'Sometimes things just don't work out,' Mum said.

I didn't know what to say.

So when I woke up in the hospital Michael was the first person I thought about. He's the only kid I'd ever known to be properly sick. And it wasn't his fault. Not at all. But this. Me ending up in a hospital bed after passing out from severe dehydration. That was my fault. There was no getting around it. If I hadn't been taking all those laxatives I never would have ended up in this situation.

I felt like an asshole.

'Laxative abuse,' stated Nurse Amy, 'can result in kidney and liver damage. You were admitted because you fainted from dehydration, a condition that can lead to death. Irritable bowel, a lazy colon, infections and even heart damage have all been associated with misusing laxatives. How are you feeling now?'

'Stupid.'

Nurse Amy was sassy and no nonsense. I guess she was about Mum's age and she had bright red hair and rockabilly eyeliner. She was probably going out dancing after work.

'You're not the first young woman to be admitted to this hospital for mistreating their body in the quest for thinness. But you know, laxatives aren't even very good for that. All they really do is get rid of water. They don't even make you lose weight.'

'Am I going to be okay? I mean, do I have kidney damage or anything?'

'We still have to wait for some test results, but my feeling is you are going to be fine. But it's not like you can go home and forget all this ever happened. Eating disorder recovery is never easy.'

'I wouldn't say I have an eating disorder. I don't even weigh myself!'

'When you go through a packet of laxatives every couple of days that is classified as an eating disorder. You're in hospital, Winter. This is serious. How long have you been taking laxatives and dieting?'

'Not that long. A few months, I guess.'

'You know it's very hard to ignore messages that tell us the skinnier the better. But a few kilos are not worth killing yourself for.'

A *few* kilos . . .

With that, Nurse Amy checked my blood pressure and said it was a bit low. 'You're probably still feeling a little light-headed. But it shouldn't take long before you start feeling better. I'll go and find you something to eat.'

And that's when my parents walked in.

'What were you thinking?' Mum demanded. 'I don't understand. Why would you do this to yourself?'

Dad looked teary and uncomfortable. 'How are you feeling, honey?' he asked kindly.

'How do you think she's feeling?' Mum piped up. 'Like shit, I expect.'

'I'm fine, just a bit tired.'

In my head I was thinking about how I was going to maintain my current size through diet and exercise alone. I was going to have to be diligent, that was for sure.

'The doctor said you can come home tomorrow. She's going to come and see you soon. Jesus, Winter.

You could have done some serious damage.'

'Is there anything you'd like us to get you?' Dad asked. I knew it was a big deal for him to be here, leaving work early and all. 'Maybe some magazines?'

'But you know you don't have to be skinny like those models, right?' Mum interrupted.

'Mum!'

Just then Nurse Amy came in with a tray of hospital food. Chicken soup and pasta followed by chocolate mousse for dessert. I made a point of eating it without making a fuss, just to show that I wasn't as messed up about food as they all thought. Besides, I was really, really hungry. It felt good to eat.

Chapter 33: Not Pretty Enough

I was out in two days, unlike Hannah the coma girl, who I discovered was in the same hospital as me. Only she wasn't going anywhere.

'It's not looking good,' Melody announced. 'If she hasn't woken up by now there's a good chance she has brain damage.'

'Shit,' I replied, feeling stupid and sad for poor Hannah, who wasn't as lucky as I was.

Melody, George and I were hanging out in my bedroom. After I passed out I made Mum tell my friends and Mabel I'd simply fainted due to low blood pressure. I also made her lie and say that I wasn't allowed visitors in the hospital. And Oliver? Well, he thought I was at home in bed with the flu.

'So what really happened?' Melody asked. 'Nobody spends two days in hospital because their blood pressure was a little bit low.'

'It's complicated,' I said, thinking I would make up a convincing story about blood sugar issues. But then I looked at George and Melody, the way they were watching me in anticipation, their brown eyes filled with concern. And I told them everything.

I could feel them staring at me as I spoke.

'Oh, Winter,' Melody said, 'I feel terrible.'

'Why?'

'We knew something wasn't right,' George said. 'We should have done something.'

'Don't be stupid, I didn't want you to know. I got pretty good at covering things up. There's nothing you could have done. Look how pissed off I got during movie night.'

'You're not going to keep taking them, are you?' Melody asked. 'Please don't. Everything is going so great for you. Lisa loved her jumpsuit, Oliver made you that tape . . .'

'Does Oliver know?' George asked.

'No way! I'm so embarrassed.'

We sat in silence.

'I keep forgetting to ask,' I said, deliberately changing the subject. 'How did you go at the modelling agency?'

'Oh God.' Melody sighed dramatically. 'I went to see that Jane woman and she said I need to get professional pictures done. And that I need to lose five kilos.'

'Can you believe it?' George sounded flabbergasted. 'How messed up is that? She's already skinny!'

Again, I'm not proud about this, but a part of me felt relieved. If even beautiful, perfect Melody isn't good enough in the eyes of modelling agents, then who is?

'What did you say?' I asked.

'I said I'm not interested. I want to be a doctor, not a model. And the last thing I need is to go on some crazy diet that makes me obsessive and unable to concentrate. No offence.'

'Totally,' I agreed. 'That's bullshit.'

Chapter 34: Guess What? My Kid's in Hospital 'cos of a Bout of Laxative Abuse

The other thing that happened when I got out of hospital was that my parents now had a new topic to fight about. Me. Or rather, who stuffed me up more – my aging, body-obsessed hipster mother or my absent, workaholic dad? It was an argument nobody would ever win.

'How long has this been going on?' Dad was asking Mum, accusingly, as I listened in to the fight they were having in the kitchen, thinking I was asleep.

'I don't know. She's been doing all that healthy eating. I thought she was just looking after herself.'

'You would think that!' Dad sounded pretty angry.

'What's that supposed to mean?'

'It means that you are always going on about your weight and now our daughter is suffering.'

'How would you even know that? You're never here.'

'Don't you dare.' Dad was *definitely* mad now. 'I work so we can have all of this.'

'Bullshit. That's what you tell yourself to justify the fact that you are a workaholic who would rather be in the office than here with us.'

It was the same old blame game but this time, I understood. It's not something you'd brag about to your friends and colleagues. 'Hey, guess what? My kid's in hospital 'cos of a bout of laxative abuse. Gave herself the shits real good'.

So of course, Mum and Dad did what any middle-class parent would do in their situation. They shipped me off to see a shrink, whom they referred to as an 'eating disorder specialist'.

I liked Rosie right away. She was in her fifties, with shoulder-length silver hair and red lipstick. She wasn't fat or skinny and wore big, statement necklaces and flowy smock dresses that looked bohemian and comfortable. She spoke softly and clearly and seemed the kind of person who managed to remain sensible and measured at all times. I liked her office. She burned essential oils and used lamps to light up the room.

Rosie already knew the basics about why I'd come to see her, but she wanted me to tell her in my own words. So I told her about my dieting and laxatives and she acted all sympathetic and kind. It wasn't until I said, 'I don't think it's that big a deal. I mean, Mum said most girls go through a phase where they throw up or starve themselves or whatever. She says it's a normal part of growing up as a woman,' that Rosie visibly recoiled and looked kind of horrified. But only for a second. Her professional therapist face soon returned, as she regained her composure.

'She may be trying to offer comfort,' Rosie firmly stated, 'and it's lovely that you are trying to understand where your mum is coming from. But Winter, it is not normal or healthy to take laxatives or throw up to try and lose weight. Your mum is not my patient and I don't know her, but it sounds to me like she has her own issues with food and weight and she has, probably unintentionally, modelled an unhealthy attitude towards food.'

'She's really skinny,' I replied.

'Why is that so important to you? Do you think being skinny is the path to happiness?'

'Well,' I considered. 'No. Yes. Maybe. I mean, I have a boyfriend now and a job and I sold an outfit to my first client. I know I'm not skinny–'

'Winter,' Rosie interrupted me. 'I think it's very important that I stop you there. Those things you just described happened in spite of your eating disorder, not because of it.'

'I'm not sure if I have an eating disorder . . .'

'You have an unhealthy relationship with food that landed you in hospital.'

'I guess.'

'Call it whatever you want, but I can tell you this. Success and your happiness come from inside. They are not weight related.'

'I suppose,' I mumbled, not entirely sure that I believed her.

'Recovery is never an easy process,' Rosie continued. 'Especially when it comes to body image and food issues. We are bombarded every day with images of how the female body is supposed to look and many of these images are unrealistic or downright fake. It's a sad fact that most of us need to fight against ridiculous standards of beauty in order to feel positive about ourselves. A lot of women find it helpful to avoid mainstream media as much as they can, especially in the early stages.'

'That makes sense,' I said, not adding that I still had doubts that I'd ever be able to accept myself.

Chapter 35: I Didn't Even Use a Spoon

Let me start by saying that Oliver's mum and my mum are *polar opposites*. In fact, I don't think it would be possible to find any two women of the same age who are so completely different in every single way.

As you know, my mum is skinny and glamorous and, let's face it, kind of vain and self-obsessed. There is no way she would have Oliver over for dinner and not wear any make-up or leave her roots completely untouched and go shamelessly frizzy and grey. Nor would Mum wear one of those long Indian skirts with bells hanging off the drawstring waist and she would definitely not give Oliver a hug upon first meeting him and act like she was his favourite aunty or something.

But that's exactly what Anita was like. Warm and dowdy and sparkly-eyed, with a kind face and not one iota of fashion sense. She definitely didn't do Botox, though I'm sure if Mum met her she would recommend she give it a shot.

'Winter,' she said, beaming, 'wonderful to meet you. Thank you so much for coming over. I know that meeting your boyfriend's mum for the first time is not exactly easy.'

'Hi.' I wasn't sure what else to say. Was I supposed to admit to being nervous, or would that be total TMI?

'Luckily for me, I never even met Oliver's dad, let alone his father's mother!'

She made me laugh. Anita was funny. I started to relax.

'Mum!' Oliver nudged his mum, whispering, 'Sorry,' in my ear.

'Oh dear,' Anita said. 'Doesn't she know about the sperm donor situation?'

'She does,' Oliver replied sternly.

'I promised I wouldn't embarrass him, you know.'

'Too late,' Oliver mumbled, but he was smiling.

Anita had made some kind of Moroccan tagine filled with chicken and olives and prunes. She told us about the homeless women she was working with and about the shelter she managed. Like Oliver, she was compassionate and kind, but sensible. She wasn't all about saving the world, even though she looked after displaced people every day. Unlike my mum, she had no idea who Bruno Mars was and she'd barely heard of the *Social Landmines* franchise or roller derby or Perez Hilton. She was earnest and warm and daggy, the kind of woman who would burn incense and buy Indian carpets and paint her lounge room bright orange, just because she felt like it one morning.

'So you and Oliver met at that dreadful party?' she asked.

'Yeah,' I answered awkwardly. How much did she know?

Everything, it turned out. Well, everything about Hannah getting drunk and falling off the balcony and ending up in a coma and almost dying. I prayed Oliver hadn't told her about the fact that I vomited into a pot plant because I was so intoxicated. He and his mum certainly seemed to be into sharing stories.

Still, while Anita had a worthy job and no interest in popular culture or fashion, she wasn't the judgemental type either. She just chatted away, asking me questions about myself like I was her equal, not just some teenage girl who happened to be dating her son. It was easy, but disarming. Anita made me feel so at ease I found myself telling her all about working for Mabel and my fashion dreams and how I was worried I didn't have what it takes to work in such an image-driven industry.

'Maybe you'll be the one to help broaden our narrow ideas about what constitutes beauty.' Anita looked me right in the eye. 'We all need talented young women like you.'

'You sound like Rosie, this lady I know.' I almost blurted out that she was my shrink, but luckily I stopped myself just in time.

‘Who’s Rosie?’ Oliver looked at me quizzically.

‘Oh, just some friend of my parents,’ I lied nervously.

‘Well, you should listen to her. Trust me. I used to work in an eating disorder clinic and I’m telling you, it was very depressing. All those wasted lives. I mean, these were clients with serious and complex mental health issues, but body image anxiety is practically forced upon all of us. It takes strength not to get caught up in that stuff, especially when you’re surrounded by it all the time.’

‘I guess,’ I muttered.

‘Now, time for dessert and a nice cup of sweet mint tea,’ Anita said cheerfully as she left the table.

‘Mum’s chocolate pudding is the best,’ Oliver said as we waited for Anita to return. ‘You’ll love it.’

‘Yum!’ I exclaimed in an enthusiastic attempt to hide the anxiety I was feeling about downing a tonne of empty calories.

Still, I forced myself to eat every single mouthful of the chocolate pudding (and ice-cream!) that was placed in front of me. It was a relief when we finished eating and Anita asked Oliver to walk me home.

‘Your mum is so nice,’ I said to Oliver as we walked through the park. ‘I had no idea.’

‘She liked you,’ Oliver replied.

‘Really?’

‘Why wouldn’t she?’ Oliver kissed me in the moonlight like a character from a cheesy romantic novel.

'Because I'm superficial and want to be a fashion designer.'

Who worries way too much about the fattening nature of desserts, I silently added.

'You're not superficial,' Oliver retorted. 'What are you talking about? You're amazing and creative and kind. I wouldn't love you if you were just some bimbo fashion girl.'

I felt confident that Oliver really liked me, so when we reached my front gate I decided to tell him everything.

'There's something I need to tell you.' It was time to tell the truth. 'Rosie is my shrink.'

'Oh.' Oliver looked perplexed. 'I didn't know you saw a shrink.'

'I just started after I came out of hospital.'

'Hospital?' He was getting super confused now.

So I told him about the laxatives, the diet, the fact that I lied to him about the flu. And it felt good, letting it all out. A relief. Now I didn't have to hide things from him anymore.

'Oh, and before we got together properly, I kind of kissed George. Just once.'

I figured I may as well lay it all on the table.

I reached for Oliver's shoulder, but he pulled back.

'Are you okay?' I asked, noticing the pissed-off look on his face.

'What am I supposed to do with all of this? Who are you?'

'Oliver, I'm sorry. I wanted to tell you, but I was ashamed.'

I tried to touch him again but he wouldn't let me.

'I've gotta go.' He turned away, cold.

'Oliver,' I pleaded.

'I'm really tired,' he said curtly. 'I'll see you later.'

And that was it. Oliver walked away without turning back. I stood, leaning against my front fence, thinking that Oliver would turn around, that he'd at least want to talk some more. But he didn't return. I checked my phone. No messages. There was nothing left for me to do but go inside.

Like a zombie, I headed straight for the fridge. Shaking, I grabbed Dad's cookie-dough ice-cream. To my relief, there was plenty left. I ate some with my fingers, not even taking the time to grab a spoon. I just dunked my hands into the cold, gooey fat-filled tub and shoved as much into my mouth as I could. Over and over again until the tub was scraped clean. I wanted more, so I searched the pantry for Mum's no-longer-secret stash. She knew how to hide her binge-eating supplies, though, because all I could find were chia seeds, quinoa and a packet of activated almonds.

Useless.

I decided to have a shower, wash it all away. I looked down at my stomach. Fat and bloated and disgusting. If there were still laxatives in the house, I would have taken them. But I had no choice but to let the pudding and ice-cream sit inside me like a punishment, reminding me of what I'd done.

'Who are you?' Oliver had asked.

I didn't know how to answer.

Chapter 36: How to Achieve a Better Body Image 101

I wasn't scheduled to see Rosie for another two weeks, but there was no way I could wait that long. So I called her. Desperate. Maybe it was because I burst into tears as soon as Rosie picked up the phone, but she let me come and see her straight away.

'I've ruined everything,' I blurted out. 'I told Oliver the truth and now he hates me and I ate an entire tub of ice-cream and I didn't even use a spoon.'

'Okay, Winter.' Rosie looked worried. 'Why don't you slow down and tell me exactly what happened?'

So I did. And it sounded so terrible I couldn't stop the tears from falling down my face.

Rosie sat and listened patiently, handing me a box of tissues so I could wipe away the tears.

When I finished, Rosie said calmly, 'You had a setback. You used food as a source of comfort and that's okay. Eating a tub of ice-cream might not be ideal, but it's not the end of the world. It's happened. Forgive yourself and let it go. Right now.'

'But what about Oliver? He hates me!'

‘Good relationships are built on trust and honesty. You told him because you needed to, because you care about him and you wanted to share your experience with him. It’s up to Oliver now. If he decides he can’t handle it, you need to accept that he isn’t the right boy for you.’

‘I guess,’ I muttered. It was okay for Rosie. She probably had a husband. Me, I was destined to be a fat virgin forever. ‘It’s just that I really, really liked him and I thought he liked me, too.’

‘I don’t know him, but it’s possible he felt betrayed by the fact that you hid so much from him.’

Not what I wanted to hear.

‘But I was embarrassed!’

‘He might need a bit of time and space,’ Rosie reassured me. ‘He’ll come back when he’s ready. And if he doesn’t, that’s his choice.’

That made me cry even harder.

But Rosie didn’t let me dwell on this. Instead, she got up and grabbed a pamphlet from her shelf. It was from some health organisation and included tips for developing a healthy body image.

‘I think you might find this useful.’

Tips on how to improve your body image

- Shut down voices in your head that tell you your body isn't good enough.
- Embrace and appreciate all the things your body can do.
- Never compare yourself to others.
- Look at media and social media with a critical eye.
- Hunt down images that depict beauty in a diverse and body-positive way.
- Surround yourself with positive people.
- Write a list of the top 5 things you like about yourself and read it everyday.
- Your weight does not define you.
- Wear clothes that make you feel great.
- Never feel guilty about eating. Enjoy your food and nourish your body.
- Treat yourself with kindness.

Rosie and I went through the pamphlet together.

'It may seem a little obvious,' Rosie said, as if sensing my scepticism, 'but a lot of clients find referring back to the list when they are feeling down really helpful.'

'I'll try,' I said to Rosie as she showed me out the door.

It's not like I had anything else to lose.

Chapter 37: The Gym

'Why don't you come to the gym with me this morning?' Mum looked at me expectantly. Even though she was wearing her perfectly coordinated Lululemon performance outfit she looked vulnerable, as if she were fearful of rejection. 'Not because I think you need to do any extra exercise,' she added quickly. 'You look great. I just thought you might like it. It's actually a lot of fun, something we can do together. I even checked with Rosie to see if it would be okay. I mean, I don't want to trigger you or anything.'

I instinctively wanted to say 'no'. I was still feeling pretty awful about the ice-cream binge two days ago, and working out with Mum at 7am was not my idea of fun at the best of times. But the look on her face was so full of hope that I couldn't help but feel that rejecting her offer would crush her spirit somehow. She was so clearly trying to reach out, connect with me by involving me in her life. Besides, I remembered the advice from Rosie's pamphlet: *Appreciate all the things your body can do*.

Of course, the other, more unhinged side of

my psyche figured it might help me lose some more weight.

'Okay.'

'Really?' Mum was so excited I thought she might start to cry. 'I even bought you some gloves, just in case.'

'Gloves?'

'Yeah. It's boxing today. We are going to have a blast.'

With her toothpick arms Mum hardly looked like boxing material. She never came home with black eyes or concussions or anything. What was she talking about?

She must have noticed the look of fear in my eyes. 'Don't worry, we don't fight each other.' She laughed. 'You just punch a bag or focus mitts. It's a seriously awesome workout. Cathartic, actually. Really good for your head. It might be just what you need.'

It was pretty obvious that Mum was a regular as soon as we entered the gym. Everyone seemed to know her. The staff, the other fitness freaks, regular-looking people in daggy shorts and what were no doubt complimentary oversized T-shirts with logos advertising telephone companies or universities or beer.

'Sienna!' said a huge, orange-hued man whose muscles bulged like walnuts. 'You've brought a guest today!'

The man's voice boomed whenever he spoke, his

teeth unnaturally white, like someone from a TV show. His head was shaved and he was covered in tattoos of birds and retro-looking women in sailor outfits and wiggle dresses. *Good God*, I couldn't help but think. *Are you and Mum having an affair?* Still, his smile seemed genuine and he acted like he was really pleased to meet me.

'Winter, this is Sebastian. As you can see, he works out. A lot.'

Sebastian grinned. 'I have heard so much about you!'

'Winter's just sold her first piece of commissioned work.' Mum was positively beaming. 'She's crazy talented.'

Was Mum showing me off? She was acting kind of weird. Proud.

'So you're working out with your mum today? She's the best.'

With that, Sebastian walked off. 'He's totally on roids,' Mum whispered to me. 'But he's a sweetheart.'

Mum took me to what seemed to be the boxing area and handed me a skipping rope.

'Now, the first thing we need to do is warm up. Like this.'

Mum skipped like she was dancing, one foot, then the next, fast, elegant and, well, impressive. I tried to copy what she was doing, but the rope kept getting tangled and it was so exhausting I thought I was going to pass out.

'Mum.' I was panting. 'How do you do this? It's so hard.'

'Don't worry,' Mum reassured me, not even puffed. 'It took me weeks to get the hang of it. Let's try it slowly. You go left, then right, left, then right . . .'

But I couldn't get my feet over the rope. They kept missing and getting all tangled.

'Let's just try without the rope,' Mum suggested. 'We'll work on the feet.'

Mum was patient. And kind. She didn't laugh or tell me I was hopeless. In fact, she kept saying things like, 'You're going great' and 'It's really hard. Nobody gets it right off the bat' and 'Awesome work'. People she knew kept coming by and saying 'hello' but they weren't able to take her focus away from me.

'I'm training my daughter,' she would say. 'She's working it like a pro.'

George, Melody and I went through a boxing/fighting movie phase last year. *Million Dollar Baby*, *The Wrestler*, *Rocky* (only the original), *Karate Kid* 1 and 2. They're great stories. All about how discipline, focus and determination can raise a person from underachiever to champion. We danced to the *Rocky* soundtrack in George's living room and expressed awe at Hilary Swank's body. But I never considered myself to be a fighter, let alone someone who would do boxing for fun. *With. Her. Mother*. Until now. There I was, throwing punches at the woman who had raised me and loved me and fought with me and made me feel like shit more than once.

And it was awesome.

Besides, Oliver still hadn't called and it made me feel better to imagine the focus mitts were his face.

'Jab, cross, jab, cross,' Mum urged. 'Come on, you've got more in you than that.'

I hit hard.

'You go, girl!' Mum beamed. 'You're a fighter.'

I'm not going to lie. It was exhausting. I punched and ducked and shuffled until I couldn't hold my arms up any longer. My shoulders ached and my back hurt. I felt like I was going to die.

'Let's cool down,' Mum said finally and we did our stretches. Afterwards we went to the café for smoothies.

'Boxing saved me when Grandma Joan died,' Mum admitted. 'I just didn't know what to do with myself.'

'I still don't get why she did it. I mean, I know she was sick, but . . .'

'You know, Winter . . .' Mum looked serious. 'I think I understand why she did what she did, but that doesn't mean it doesn't suck. I will never do anything like that to you. I know I'm not the best mum in the world. But I promise, I am going to try and be better. And I'll never, ever top myself.'

Silence.

I looked down. It was terrible, not funny at all, but still. I could feel the laughter brewing, bubbling to the surface like some kind of insidious molten lava. Mum and I sat in silence. But then it started. She let out a snort, then a giggle and before we knew it, we were laughing so hard my banana smoothie came out my nose and tears dripped from my eyes.

'Here's to my mother.' Mum raised her protein power smoothie.

'To Grandma Joan.'

And we laughed again. We must have looked like two crazy people and when Sebastian sauntered by, this time dripping with sweat, he said, 'Looks like you ladies are having a good time.'

'Yes,' Mum said. 'We are.'

'Oh, Mum,' I said, once we'd calmed down. 'I'm sorry.'

'What for?'

'For all the crap I put you and Dad through. You know, ending up in hospital and everything.'

'Jesus, Winter. Never be sorry for that. I'm just so happy you have been able to push through it. I'm proud of you, you know. I'm the one who should be sorry.'

I shrugged.

'No. I should be. I guess, deep down, I've always felt the need to prove myself and the way I do that has always been through how I look. And that's wrong. It's sad, actually.'

'Well . . .' I wasn't sure what to say. I was shocked by Mum's honesty.

'And Winter, I love you, I'm so sorry that I've passed my shit onto you. Even today, maybe this wasn't a good idea. I just want you to know, I'm not trying to help you lose weight or anything. I just thought, you know, maybe boxing would help you like it helped me. You're perfect how you are.'

'Huh?' I couldn't believe my ears.

'Gosh. If only I were half the woman you are already, and you're only sixteen!'

'Okay, Mum. This is getting a bit daytime TV.'

'Sorry.' Mum laughed. 'So tell me. What did you think of boxing? Have I converted you?'

'It was great.' I was actually telling the truth. 'Mum, you were the best. Seriously, you should be a trainer.'

'Well, actually.' Mum smiled shyly. 'There is something I wanted to talk to you about.'

It was the first time since I could really remember that Mum and I had a conversation that was effortless. She told me all about how she'd started a Science degree when she finished high school, but that she'd never completed it. So now Mum was about to enrol in a Bachelor of Food and Nutrition Sciences, and she was also planning to become a certified personal trainer and group fitness instructor.

'I've been a housewife for a long time,' she told me. 'And don't get me wrong, Winter, there is no more important job than raising a family. But I need to branch out.'

'Go, Mum,' I said. 'I think that's amazing.'
'You do?' she asked.
'Are you kidding? It's awesome.'
And I meant it, I really did.

Chapter 38: Out There

'Seriously, Winter. Are you not a twenty-first century teenager? Why don't you have a blog and Instagram already?'

Mabel and I were tidying up the shop at the end of a busy Saturday. I was stressed out because three of Lisa's friends had ordered jumpsuits and I was scared I'd stuff everything up. Being busy, however, was a relief. It had been a whole week and Oliver hadn't called. I almost texted him one night, but Melody stopped me.

'He's the one who walked away,' Melody insisted. 'So leave it up to him. I'm deleting his number from your phone right now.'

'No!'

But before I could stop her, she'd grabbed my phone and the damage was done.

'Look, you know you can sew,' Mabel said, interrupting my thoughts. 'You know you can design. You need to put yourself out there. The summer break's coming up. You've got time. Three orders is nothing. You'll be done in a week.'

'I guess I could get Melody to model for me.'

'Get your friends and use yourself. You're cute. People love to see the designer behind the label.'

The thought of plastering photos of myself online was terrifying beyond comprehension. I wasn't so concerned about showing people my work, but showing people my body? I hadn't binged since the night of my fight with Oliver, but I was pretty sure I'd gained a bit of weight. Getting dressed up and posing in front of a camera? That was about as appealing as slow dancing with Mirko Palovich to Celine Dion. Besides, I was supposed to be getting all body positive and the very real possibility of having Internet trolls telling me that I look like a pork chop on legs wasn't exactly empowering. Plus-size girls who exude confidence and self-acceptance were all well and good, but I doubted I'd be jumping on that bandwagon. I just didn't have it in me.

Rosie, on the other hand, thought it was a great idea.

'If you want to work in fashion you need to put yourself out there,' Rosie insisted. 'Besides, I think you might be surprised by the response you receive.'

'But what if people tell me I look fat and hideous?'

'So what if they do?' Rosie said. 'Do you really care what some jealous, snotty-nosed teenager on the Internet thinks of you?'

Yes! I wanted to respond. But I wasn't in the mood for getting into a conversation about why I care so much about what others think of me, so I just said,

'I guess you're right,' in a lame attempt to convince Rosie I agreed with her.

But still, I did it. And I made George and Melody join me.

I spent an hour getting ready for my first photo shoot. I'd piled on the make-up and grabbed a pair of ridiculously high, pointy black stilettos from Mum's wardrobe. My flamingo print jumpsuit contrasted with the pleather leggings and an oversized shirt dress Melody wore, while George modelled a reconstructed tuxedo from Savers. George and Melody really got into it, posing and mucking around and laughing so hard they could barely breathe. I, on the other hand, felt like a complete douchebag.

'I feel like an idiot,' I declared.

'Lighten up,' George said, striking a pose. 'You look hot.'

You've got to put yourself out there, I kept telling myself. *Block out the voices that tell you you're not good enough. Accept that you may no longer have a boyfriend.*

I plastered on a fake smile and stood to the side, my chin pointed upwards, my hands resting on my hips in order to ensure skinnier looking arms. Online research taught me that standing front on with your arms by your sides equals tuckshop arms.

The next day I showed the photos to Mabel.

'Wow,' she declared. 'You all look fab. Who's that girl?'

'Oh, that's my friend Melody. She was scouted

by a modelling agency but they said she needed to lose five kilos, so she turned them down. Isn't she beautiful?'

'God, we still have such a long way to go. She's hot,' Mabel said. 'Do you think the two of you would be interested in doing some photo shoots for me? And I have a runway show coming up for fashion week.'

I almost fell over.

'Are you serious?'

'It's a paid gig, of course,' Mabel continued. 'I can show you both how to walk the runway.'

'You want me on the runway?'

'Absolutely,' Mabel said. 'Fashion needs diverse beauty.'

Me. Modelling. With Melody.

'I don't mind if you just pick Melody. I won't be offended. It's not like I haven't figured out that she's way better looking.'

'No, I think I want both of you. I was going to ask you anyway, and now that I've seen Melody, I love the Eurasian vibe she has going on.'

Inside I was squealing, but I did my best to act cool and calm while Mabel sat down and put the photos up on my Instagram account and new blog.

'You just need to set up an online shop and post regularly. Twice a week is good.'

And it all happened. Just like that. I was putting myself out there, no matter what.

Chapter 39: It's Been a Whole Month Since My Last Binge . . .

I never thought I'd say this, but boxing with Mum was getting me through every day I didn't hear from Oliver. I still counted calories, but I hadn't binged for a whole month and I was even beginning to accept that I had been dumped, although I continued to check my phone every half hour just in case I'd missed a call or a text. My plan was to try and use boxing as a way of appreciating what my body could do, which turned out to be more than I had expected. Boxing also tired me out, which helped me sleep instead of lying in bed every night crying and listening to that mix tape that was now more sad than funny and romantic. It burnt extra calories, too, of course, but I tried not to focus on that part.

The holidays were going fast and it wouldn't be long before Melody, George and I were in our final year of high school. Everything was beginning to feel a little more serious. We were growing up and it was actually starting to matter which subjects we chose and whether our grades were any good. I'd really let things slip last year. With the dieting and laxatives I had been so tired and focused on my weight loss that I hadn't really made much effort with schoolwork. This year I knew I had to do better. We all did. But George, in particular, was freaking out.

'My parents are threatening to send me to a private school or one of those private boys' schools,' he dramatically declared. 'If I don't get straight A's first term I'm gone.'

'We'll study together,' Melody reassured him. 'If I don't do well I'm not getting into medicine.'

'You should apply for special consideration,' I said. 'You've had a tumultuous home life, with your mum in jail and all.'

'I'm not some charity case,' Melody replied defensively. 'Winter, what's going on with Oliver? Have you heard from him at all?'

'Not a word. I'm dumped,' I said.

George's eyes narrowed. 'He's an idiot!'

'I did lie to him about everything. I probably shouldn't have told him that I kissed you.'

'What did you do that for?' Melody looked incredulous. 'It's not like George is a threat.'

'Hey!' George said.

'Well, you are *gay*.' I laughed. 'I stuffed everything up. Oliver no doubt thinks I'm a psycho. I'm trying to practise self-acceptance. I will remain single forever.'

'I wouldn't say psycho,' Melody said drolly.

'Anyway, guess who messaged me on Facebook last night?' I said, quickly changing the subject.

'Katy Perry?' George mocked.

'Very funny. No. Mirko Palovich!'

'Who's that again?' Melody asked.

'Remember that boy who called me a short, fat dog on school camp?'

'Oh yeah, that jerk.'

'Well, he sent me a PM saying *UR hot. Wanna hook up.*'

I showed them the message on my phone.

'What a loser!' Melody and George were laughing so hard they could barely breathe.

At first I thought the message was from some random weirdo/stranger. You know, the types who don't know how to use Tinder or who like looking for gullible teenage girls they might be able to rape or murder. But then I recognised the photo. A puffy-faced teenage boy wearing a Jim Beam hat, his squinty little eyes peering back at me. He was no stranger.

Mirko Palovich.

I sure wasn't sorry to see Mirko go when he and his family moved to the outer suburbs after Year 6. Mirko was so proud of what he considered to be a massive upgrade, bragging to everybody that he was moving to a mansion with its own private cinema and butler's pantry. For some reason Mirko thought the butler's pantry was a standout feature, talking down to us once he realised that nobody even knew what a butler's pantry was.

'It's like a second kitchen,' he explained condescendingly, 'where you can prepare meals for your guests but they don't see all the mess.'

'Ha! Who's going to want to be entertained by you?' scoffed his mate, James.

'Shut up!' Mirko punched James on the arm.

Looking at the photo I could see that puberty hadn't changed Mirko in any dramatic way. He was still kind of dumb-looking, though his acne appeared to have turned cystic. A fact that made me happier than it probably should have.

'I haven't replied yet,' I told them. 'I need a really good comeback.'

'How about, "I wouldn't hook up with you if you were the last boy on earth, you pimply little maggot"!' Melody said.

'Subtle.' George smirked.

'But effective,' Melody said.

'I was thinking of just saying something like, "No thanks".'

'That's a bit boring,' said George.

'But I don't want it to sound like I'm all bitter.'

'But you are!' George said.

It wasn't until I went boxing with Mum the following morning that I figured out the perfect response. Boxing does that to you. It clears your mind while releasing stress and repressed aggression. A perfect combination when Mirko Palovich is involved.

'Hello Mirko', I wrote. 'I hope you are enjoying your butler's pantry. I have been recently dumped, but even that doesn't make me desperate enough to hook up with a loser like you, not even on the rebound. In fact, I would rather spend the rest of my life perving at Justin Bieber mugshots than be within a five-kilometre radius of your maggoty face. Insert poo emoji'.

Chapter 40: Perfect Is Boring

I may be short. I may have legs like a corgi and cellulite on my thighs and wonky boobs. But there I was, standing backstage with six other models, preparing to walk out in front of at least sixty people I didn't know to showcase Mabel's latest collection: Under the Stars.

I'm not going to lie. When you're modelling in a fashion show it's hard not to be self-conscious about how you look.

Melody and I were hanging out in my room the night before our modelling debut. I'd pinched some of Mum's ridiculously expensive sheet masks so we could give ourselves facials.

'I've gained so much weight,' I lamented, looking at Melody, who resembled a serial killer with the white mask on her face. 'My BMI is off the charts.'

'Shut up.' Melody slapped me on the shoulder. 'You look amazing and everyone knows the BMI is a load of hogwash. Did you know that the BMI deems most AFL players obese?'

'Seriously?' I said. 'That actually makes me feel better.'

'It's true. You've got to start listening to that therapist of yours. You don't want to end up in hospital again, do you?'

Melody's tell-it-like-it-is approach is too much for some, but I find it comforting.

'Well. The bed was pretty comfy in there . . .'

'Don't even joke about it,' Melody said. 'You're not tempted to use again, are you?'

'I wasn't on drugs. Trust me. Enforced diarrhoea is not addictive.'

'Then what was with all the laxative abuse?'

'I guess it made me feel lighter. Like I was getting rid of all the excess calories. Even though I wasn't.'

'That makes sense.' Melody paused. 'Kind of. It's pretty gross.'

'You don't have to tell me that,' I replied. 'That is one thing I'd never do again.'

'Good.' Melody seemed satisfied. 'Now, let's watch *Gilmore Girls* on Netflix.'

Which is what we did until we were so exhausted we fell asleep.

On the day of the show I was so nervous, the make-up artist, who was Mabel's childhood friend, Renee, had to keep mattifying my shiny face with powder. Melody was even worse and kept saying that she felt like she was about to vomit. I don't know what she was worried about. While I was all 'Runway to *Real*way', Melody looked like an actual model in her floaty silver gown, braided hair and blue lips. Mabel had decided to put me in some black, star-print body-con number that she said 'showed off my curves'. The other models included Mabel's mum, two professional models from a 'plus size agency' who looked like they were only a size 12 and Tor, Mabel's gazelle-like sixteen-year-old cousin.

'You'll do great,' said one of the tall professionals standing beside me. 'Seriously, there's not much to it. You watch *Top Model* and they try and make out that modelling is as complicated as rocket science. But all you have to do is walk, turn around and walk back. And act like you mean it.'

It was easy for her to say. She was probably used to sauntering down runways in six-inch heels while everybody stared at her.

'Oh, and don't trip over,' she said, until she saw my face turn white. 'Just kidding.'

The music started. It was an original soundtrack composed by Mabel's fiancé. I was on third, after Mabel's mum and before Melody. George, James and my parents were in the audience. Mum was so proud and excited she'd been bragging about my foray into modelling to everyone at the gym. She brought along the expensive and rarely used camera Dad gave her for Christmas two years ago so she could document every single moment.

A moment that was unlikely to happen ever again.

I stood behind the stage waiting for my turn. I was relieved Mabel's mum was ahead of me. In her fifties and fatter than me, I figured she'd make me look good.

Wrong.

As she pranced out in her pink tulip skirt, all sass and attitude, the audience cheered. At the end of the runway she paused, all eyes on her, without a hint of self-consciousness. She was a goddess, so confident she may as well have been Gigi Hadid, but without that scowly pout. Shit. Now I was really under pressure.

If this was a straight-to-video Disney tween movie this would be the part where I take a deep breath, pull back my shoulders and own it. It's the part where I begin a career in front of the camera, where I surprise myself with my innate talent for performance and my charismatic personality. Where I'm spotted by a talent scout and become an unlikely media sensation, the envy of all who know me.

Naturally, that's not what happened.

I did my best. I walked to the end, smiled, turned and walked back. It was excruciating, having all those people checking me out.

It's about the clothes, not you, I kept saying to myself. *Perfect is boring*, I repeated, remembering what Rosie had said during our last session. I thought about all the *Project Runway* episodes I've watched and how I don't remember a single model, how they all just blur into one tall, skinny, top-knotted entity. Besides, I figured it was pretty obvious that I was just a regular person included in the show in a heavy-handed attempt to give the fashion industry the finger, rather than an industry professional.

In spite of her statuesque figure, Melody wasn't a whole lot better. Sure, she looked amazing, but you could tell she wasn't feeling it as she walked to the end of the runway and back without elegance, like she was in a hurry to get out of there. Her nervous expression made her look pissed off, and not in a cool way. Being so good-looking, with a natural resting bitch face, Melody's genuine kindness and concern for others was often concealed, meaning that people who didn't know her often thought she was stuck-up and arrogant. On the catwalk, nervous and unsure, this unintentional look of indifference was only heightened. Melody sure looked like she had better places to be.

'Glad that's over,' she whispered to me as she entered the backstage area.

'Tell me about it,' I said. 'I'll stick to designing.'

But Mabel still told Melody and me that we'd done a great job at the end of show cocktail party. She'd scored enough orders to fill the next six months and the media couldn't get enough of her decision to put a diverse range of ages and body types on her runway. Everyone told us how beautiful we looked.

'It shouldn't be groundbreaking, having models who aren't all fifteen and a size zero,' Mabel lectured a reporter. 'Fashion is for everyone and every woman is beautiful. I know that's been made pretty clear tonight.'

I was about to join George and James, who were holding hands and chatting to a hot male journalist about *The Bachelor*, when I felt a tap on the shoulder.

Oliver.

We hadn't talked for ages. I hadn't even been able to Internet stalk him because he never bothered to post on Facebook. It was almost like he'd done a Richard Simmons.

'What are you doing here?' I blurted out, sounding angrier than I intended.

Oliver looked sheepish.

'You know I have a thing for indie fashion. Besides, I follow you on Instagram.'

He smiled, but I wasn't in the mood so I just raised my left eyebrow, a nifty trick I spent hours perfecting when I was eight years old.

'I've really missed you,' he said, looking at the ground. 'God. I'm so nervous.'

Part of me was beyond happy to see Oliver. I wanted to hug him and say everything was fine and that I totally understood why he was pissed off and that I shouldn't have lied to him. But I couldn't bring myself to say it because I was angry. Furious, in fact. I was just beginning to accept that it was over between us. And now here he was. At this fashion show, of all places.

Oliver continued to stare at the ground. 'Can we get out of here? Go for a walk?'

'A walk?'

Oliver's face dropped and I almost felt sorry for him. Still, I waited a few seconds before reluctantly agreeing. 'All right.'

We walked through the back streets of Brunswick, the sky clear and full of stars. Oliver didn't try to hold my hand. I desperately wanted to reach out to take his, but I didn't. I stumbled a couple of times, my ridiculously high heels not easy to navigate over the uneven footpath.

'I know I messed up,' Oliver said. 'I was just so shocked. I had no idea. I felt like an idiot.'

'You felt like an idiot? Why?' I said.

'Because if something like that happened to me, I would tell you. I guess you didn't trust me.'

'It's not that,' I blurted. 'I was embarrassed. I thought you wouldn't like me if you knew. And I was right.'

Oliver didn't give me the reassurance I was after. Instead, he changed the subject.

'And isn't George gay, by the way?'

'One of my many mistakes.'

We continued in silence.

'So, you and George?'

I laughed. 'Are you kidding me? There is no way in the world. Not a chance.'

'Good,' Oliver replied. 'Because I missed you. Seriously missed you. These past months have sucked. I kept wanting to call you, but I was scared that you would never want to speak to me again. And I guess I was a bit jealous. I'm really sorry.'

'Really?'

'Yes, you dork. I don't know anybody else who appreciates analogue technology the way you do. I can't throw that away.'

'It's true. I'm sorry, too. I shouldn't have lied. I should have trusted you.'

'Yep, you should have. You're lucky I love you so much.'

'You love me?' I couldn't believe it.

'Well, yeah,' Oliver mumbled. We were facing each other now, the street empty and badly lit. But I could see his sparkly green eyes and his cute messy haircut.

'I guess I love you, too.'

And that's when we kissed, in the middle of the street, like no one else existed in the whole entire world. And when Oliver put his hands on my waist, I forced myself not to worry about my fat rolls or the cellulite that peppered my thighs or my wonky boobs and corgi legs.

Maybe the part of me that dreams of being skinnier will never go away, not completely. But that night I made a decision. I wasn't going to let my body image hang-ups ruin the rest of my life. I was going to enjoy moments like this. I was going to be me. Not perfect. Not skinny. But good enough. Actually, better than good enough. Because perfect is boring and that's not something that I am.

www.ingramcontent.com/pod-product-compliance
Lightning Source LLC
LaVergne TN
LVHW092002080726
842905LV00026B/197
9781925272772